Advance Praise for
TRAVEL WISE, TRAVEL SAFE

"Mary clearly communicates the necessary steps for anyone regardless of age or lifestyle to have the freedom to explore, discover, and connect with our world with confidence. No detail has been left out."

—Marcella Dickinson, Travel Writer

"Travel provides opportunities for increasing our knowledge and understanding of people and places. The world needs more aware, prepared, intelligent, and open-minded travelers. Mary's book provides the tips, hints, and information to gain the utmost from your travels."

—Daphne Lowe Kelley, Australia Chapter President
International Institute for Peace through Tourism

"As it becomes increasingly imperative that we bridge the gaps between hearts, minds, and cultures through international travel, Mary Long's commonsense advice on how to protect oneself against petty crime, terrorism, health hazards, and accidents is welcome and exceedingly timely."

—Louis L'Amore, President
International Institute for Peace through Tourism

"An invaluable resource for every person who travels to a new destination. Mary encourages all visitors to discover how important it is to understand and communicate with people of different cultures—one of the greatest contributions an individual can make to peace in our global community and to the tourism industry."

—Professor Sharr Prohaska, Director Undergraduate Program
Tisch Center for Hospitality, Tourism and Travel Administration
New York University

D1519141

"I wish I'd had this book ten years ago, but thank god it's here now! There isn't a traveler today who hasn't experienced travel mishaps, illnesses, and unpleasantries that could have been avoided by thinking, behaving, and planning differently. This book shows us how to do that."

—Gregory J.P. Godek, author
1001 Ways to Be Romantic

"With so many tips for every type of travel, circumstance, and traveler, this unique guide makes a necessary and valuable addition to everyone's travel library."

—Sarafina Saunders, Owner
Frigate Books, New York

TRAVEL WISE

~~~~~~~~~~~~~~~~

TRAVEL SAFE

TRAVEL WISE

from one who's been there and back

TRAVEL SAFE

Mary Long Harvey

Travel Resource Center

TRAVEL WISE, TRAVEL SAFE.

FIRST EDITION

ISBN 0-9666733-1-X

10 9 8 7 6 5 4 3 2 1

I dedicate this book to the living memory of four very special people. To my sister, Colleen Sabri, who was my first international travel cohort; to my mother and father, Simon and Patricia Barker; and to the best travel companion ever, my husband, Paul A. Harvey. Though they have left our physical world, they have nevertheless been the biggest force of inspiration for me to get this book out to the public at such a critical time in our history.

———————————————————————

Contents

Acknowledgments   *xiii*

Introduction   *xv*

1   The Travel Decision   1
Some Key Questions to Get You Started

2   Making Travel Preparations   11
Planning a Safe and Healthy Trip

3   In Transit   39
What Could Go Wrong and How to Prevent It

4   Arriving at Your Destination   61
Making the Best of Your Vacation

5   The New Millennium Travel Agent   89
What They Do, and Why You Still Need Them

6   Top Tips for Traveling Solo   99

7   Top Tips for Traveling with Children   107

8   Top Tips for Business Travel   117

9   Top Tips for Lifestyle and Specialty Travel   123

10   Top Tips for Elderly and Disability Travel   129

11   Top Tips for Traveling with Pets   137

12   Top Tips for Healthy Travel   143

Appendix   *149*

Donate for Peace   *169*

Acknowledgments

From the depths of my heart and soul, I thank the thousands of people too numerous to name for encouraging me to bring this timely book to print. You are a vast combination of clients, students, associate professors, authors, speakers, travel industry executives and professionals, mentors, friends, and family.

I want to especially thank those whom I've never met, yet who have shared their travel experiences by attending my radio, television, and teleclass seminars from all over the globe. Together we have made a great contribution to this world.

Special thanks to Gail Bradney, editor, whose insight, experience, and magic has made this entire project come together, and without whom this book would not have been possible. Thanks to Elizabeth Cline, layout and design; Nanette Clapper, Oakridge Travel Medical Clinic; my mentor, Joanne McCall, McCall Public Relations, for offering the greatest encouragement to get this book done; Captain Anders Anderson, *SS Universe,* for his trade secrets about what really goes on behind the scenes on luxury liners; Barbara D. Allen, Passage International, Inc., for being the best travel agent I've ever known and for sending me pertinent, timely articles that added immensely to this project; Jody Stevenson, The Anam Center, for her ongoing guidance and encouragement; Don Wright, Don Wright Productions, my speaking coach who helped me fine-tune my best keynote speech; and Ronald Scott Irwin, for his editing and research.

Introduction

In February 2003, I had the honor of attending the Second Global Summit on Peace through Tourism, in Geneva, Switzerland, as part of the Educators Forum. Organized by the International Institute for Peace through Tourism, in partnership with the World Travel and Tourism Council, the summit came at a most opportune time for me.

Just prior to completing my book, I wanted to get a global perspective and better understanding of how other nations and other cultures are coping with world fear and uncertainty toward traveling outside our own comfort zones. One of my ongoing missions as a travel educator has been to find a way to ease the anxieties and fears of people who travel in all parts of the world.

The summit experience proved to be a real eye-opener for me and confirmed what I have long believed and taught: that each and every one of us who packs a suitcase can be an instrument of peace and kindness. If we stay home, living as hostages, not contributing to the world economies that rely on our tourism and travel dollars, we will be bending to the will of groups that do not want our world to be one world, of one heart.

On the other hand, by venturing out and getting to know other cultures, you become a goodwill ambassador for your people. Every time you learn about another culture, you enrich yourself and all those around you.

I have found that the key to traveling without fear and anxiety is to be informed and prepared. By doing homework and research about your destination, you gain a better understanding of the culture, the country, and the customs of the area you will visit. Foreknowledge is your best travel companion. The other part of the formula is to prepare, plan, and pack the essential items that will make your trip a success and will insure that you remain healthy and safe the whole time you are away from home.

When people congratulate me on the good timing of this book, I have to chuckle. I have literally been researching this book for years! Having traveled all over the world as a seminar leader and travel writer and speaker, I have picked up a thing or two about expecting the unexpected. I know firsthand what it is like to live in the heart of the Middle East, exotic Iran, and in the heart of American culture, San Francisco. I have good friends in more than forty countries. Through all of my years as a travel expert, I have never felt that there has been a greater need to pay attention to safety when traveling than there is right now.

The goal of this book is to help all of us travel with ease and confidence, and to learn better ways to connect with our world.

I designed the book so it is easy to use. Chapter One begins with your initial decision to travel and helps train your brain to start thinking in a new way, with safety and health in the forefront. Chapter Two walks you through various planning and preparation phases for different modes of travel and different types of trips. Chapter Three accompanies you on your trip, offering insider tips and hints for preventing or dealing with every possible thing that could go wrong in transit. In Chapter Four, you have arrived at your destination, where I help you avoid still more perils and potential mishaps. Chapter Five sings the praises of travel agents in our new millennium, and demonstrates why travelers in our uncertain world need their services now more than ever.

The last seven chapters of the book are my top tips for various types of travelers and travel scenarios. These are gems of wisdom I have compiled over the course of decades as a travel educator and writer.

Throughout, I have peppered the pages with my own travel anecdotes, lest you think I have never used bad judgment, been ill-prepared, or been the victim of a crime myself, as well as dozens of my favorite tips, hints, tricks, checklists, bits of advice, and jewels of common sense.

As this book goes to press, I see our world changing rapidly, and with it, the travel climate. For updated travel tips that reflect current news and events around the world, and for a perspective on how these might affect your safety and security as a tourist and traveler, please visit my website frequently, at www.travelresourcecenter.com.

I hope this book helps you become a more confident traveler. I leave you, below, with the International Institute for Peace through Tourism's "Credo of the Peaceful Traveler."

Grateful for the opportunity to travel and
experience the world, and because peace
begins with the individual, I affirm my
personal responsibility and commitment to:

- Journey with an open mind and gentle heart
- Accept with grace and gratitude the diversity
  I encounter
- Revere and protect the natural environment that
  sustains all life
- Appreciate all cultures I discover
- Respect and thank my hosts for their welcome
- Offer my hand in friendship to everyone I meet
- Support travel services that share these views
  and act upon them
- By my spirit, words, and actions, encourage
  others to travel the world in peace

A portion of the profits from this book will be donated to the development of a West Coast chapter of the International Institute for Peace through Tourism. Wishing you safe, healthy, and enjoyable travel experiences from here on out.

Peace,
Mary Long Harvey

Have a great trip!
Bon Voyage! French
Kalo Taxidi! Greek
Gute Reise! German
¡Buen viaje! Spanish
Buon viaggio! Italian
Boa viagem! Portuguese
Good day, Mate! (Guess what country?)

1
The Travel Decision
Some Key Questions to Get You Started

Lots of things begin racing through your head when you first consider taking a trip. If you are like most of us, your thoughts jump ahead to what you will pack, things to buy beforehand, loose ends you need to tie up before leaving. You may already be imagining yourself lounging at the beach in sunglasses, sipping a cool drink, or maybe strolling through an ancient archaeological site like millions before you.

Stop! This is the best advice I can give you. Instead, find a time to sit down in a quiet place with a pen and pad, and take a few moments to ask yourself some key questions to get you thinking about comfort, health, and safety. Conscious thought before taking a trip is the best way to prevent disaster later on.

This book is chock-full of tips, checklists, and specific recommendations to help you avoid just about every situation that can arise once you leave home, and to help you cope with unpleasant and unexpected circumstances that are bound to occur no matter how well you have planned. *My goal is to show you how to expect the unexpected when traveling at home or abroad.*

In this first chapter, I want you to focus on getting into your pre-trip mindset. After that, you will be in the right frame of mind to pay attention to all of the tips and details about smart booking, packing, and preparation that begin in Chapter 2.

From One Who Has Been There and Back

I always tell people that the world is my office. I make my living by traveling and passing along my experiences to others. I have spent time in thirty-eight countries worldwide, have flown on hundreds of airplanes—commercial, chartered, and private. I have been on domestic trains, buses, and public transportation in almost every major U.S. city, and have had the pleasure of crisscrossing Europe on those wonderfully efficient and romantic trains and ferries. I have rented countless vehicles worldwide. I cannot begin to count the number of cruise ships on which I have been a happy passenger, either lecturing aboard or on vacation. I have even had delightful experiences on balloons, rickshaws, camels, and elephants. Between professional travel experience and my years as a travel agent, travel author, and lecturer, I have learned some valuable secrets about how to travel safely and successfully.

I have also been the victim of many travel mishaps: stolen or missing luggage, luggage break-ins, muggings, car breakdowns, illness in unfamiliar cities, airport terminal hassles, road rage incidents, foreigner hostility, scary situations, and more. I have included many of these personal stories in the book because they will help you, as they did me, understand what could happen when you travel. More important, they will get you thinking about safety and health. What I can say without hesitation is this: *Most things that go wrong when you travel are avoidable.* That is where planning and good sense come into play.

Take it from one who has been there and back: The very best way to create an exceptional travel experience is to plan wisely and carefully beforehand. Start by asking yourself the following questions to get into a travel-savvy state of mind.

What Is the Purpose of My Trip?

Is this a trip for business or for pleasure? Or is its purpose to fulfill an obligation, such as attending a wedding or bar mitzvah, or to pay a visit to an elderly parent or an ailing friend? The purpose of your trip and your destination will dictate everything from what to pack and how to budget, to your mode of transportation and how long you will stay.

Business trips are the easiest to plan. I always say if you could plan vacations the way you plan business trips, you would have the most successful travel experiences. A business trip is plotted out from beginning to end, with free time and downtime served up in precise portions between meetings and business meals, like slices of rich dessert. With business trips, you know your budget and you pack just the right amount of clothes. Try to adopt that same organized, structured attitude toward all trips from here on out.

How Long Do I Plan to Be Away?

When considering your trip, set definite departure and return times if possible. Be realistic about the amount of time you want to spend away from home. Consider pressing obligations left behind by you and any travel companions. Find the amount of time that feels "right"—not too long and just long enough. Long trips require more money, more luggage, and more pre-trip preparation and arrangements. Although "grown-up homesickness" is seldom acknowledged or talked about, it is important to consider at this planning stage, especially if you will be traveling alone.

How Much Can I Really Afford?

If you do not have the finances to support your dream trip, then wait until you do. I say this because if you are too frugal, you will end up sacrificing safety. When you do not have enough money, you tend to stay in cheaper, less desirable hotels, or you book off-brand rental cars, or use travel companies that are out to scam you. *You get what you pay for.* I simply cannot express this fact enough.

Keeping this in mind, work out a budget you can live with—how much you can comfortably spend on transportation, lodging, meals, luxuries, and souvenirs. On vacation, we always spend a little more than expected; it is just a rule of thumb. Remember to budget for emergencies such as medicine, unexpectedly long layovers, and lost belongings you might have to replace.

Who Will Be Traveling with Me?

Traveling with children, elderly companions, or people with disabilities necessitates a different kind of planning, as does traveling solo. Focus some good, hard thought on your travel companions. Will you be with young children who have difficulty sitting still? Will you have a travel companion who gets off-kilter when he or she does not eat precisely on schedule? Does anyone accompanying you have special needs or require certain medications or medical devices? Will you be bringing a pet?

What Mode of Travel Will I Use?

The two factors that are typically front and center when deciding *how* you are going to travel are time and money. Let us take a look at some of the other pros and cons of various modes of travel.

Car Travel

Pros. Driving your own car has distinct advantages. You are familiar with your car's quirks and abilities. Too, driving is almost always the cheapest way to go, particularly when you are traveling with one or more companions. It is the easiest way to travel with pets. Driving also affords you the most flexibility in terms of stopping, resting, or finding diversions along the way.

Renting a car can be great, since it saves wear and tear on your own vehicle. These days, rentals have wonderful amenities, such as global positioning systems (GPS) that can help you find your way in a strange

> **Chances of Accidental Death:**
>
> By motor vehicle:
> 1 in 6,300
>
> By railway:
> 1 in 242,000
>
> By commercial air:
> 1 in 1,568,000
>
> Source: Nat'l Highway Traffic Safety Adm.

city. Rental car companies always have special deals and discounts for smart travelers who know the right questions to ask.

Cons. Unfortunately, driving is the *least* safe way to travel. The most recent statistics available from the Federal Highway Administration report a whopping 6,356,000 car accidents in the United States in 2000. About 3.2 million involved injuries and 41,821 deaths. About 95 percent of all transportation deaths occur on our nation's highways, which is where you will be.

When driving, two of the most important considerations to keep in mind are traffic and weather. If you will be traveling during a holiday, the risks of accidents or delays skyrocket. So, too, in inclement weather.

Top Ten States for Motor Vehicle Fatalities in 2000:	
1. Texas	3,769
2. California	3,753
3. Florida	2,999
4. Georgia	1,541
5. Pennsylvania	1,520
6. North Carolina	1,472
7. New York	1,458
8. Illinois	1,418
9. Michigan	1,382
10. Ohio	1,351

Source: www.car-accidents.com

If driving your own car, consider how much wear it will put on your own vehicle. You may not see the extra expense now, but you could down the road. Rental cars can be pricy and are generally more dangerous, since you are operating a vehicle with which you are unfamiliar, with different "blind" spots than your own car, different steering and braking capabilities, and less reliability.

Recreational Vehicle (RV) Travel

Pros. RV travel, also known as motor home travel, is on the rise. There are approximately 16,000 RV-friendly campgrounds in the United States, half of them private, and the rest in national and state parks and forests. Campground facilities vary greatly and the cost per night is dependent on many factors. Facilities commonly found at campgrounds include: electric, water, and sewage hook-ups; washing machines and dryers; swimming pools; recreation rooms; playgrounds; and on-site convenience stores. The cost of camping beats any hotel or motel, typically between $10 and $50 a night.

Across North America, and particularly in Europe, RV parks in wonderful locations with great amenities are springing up faster than dandelions. This is a great way to travel with children, elderly, and disabled companions. It is a terrific mode of travel if you want to bring your pet. And it is a great way to go when you have plenty of time, want to see a lot of sights, and want to have full control over where and when to stop for sightseeing and other diversions. A popular trend these days is to use an RV for business and combine it with a family vacation. Most RV agencies offer drive/fly packages, which let you drive one way and then fly back home. The cheapest way to travel is to take advantage of the off-peak and other money-saving specials that RV agencies run regularly.

Cons. RV rental agencies offer good deals here and especially in Europe, where renting a motor home is much cheaper. But rates soar during peak summer tourism months. Like automobile travel, traffic and weather pose risks. When renting an RV, you may end up paying unexpected "gotchas" at the end of your trip if you do not ask the right questions and do your homework ahead of time.

Regional Gas Prices, Listed from Most to Least Expensive:

1. West Coast
2. New England
3. Mid-Atlantic
4. Rocky Mountains
5. Midwest
6. Southeast
7. Gulf Coast

Time of Year When Gasoline Prices Are Typically Highest:

Summer

Average Rate of Summer Gas Increase:

+6 cents/gallon

Source: U.S. Dept. of Energy Statistics

Bus/Motorcoach Travel

Pros. Commercial buses are the "people's" transportation. The best thing they have going for them is that they are inexpensive. With private, or chartered buses, known as motorcoaches, your bus mates will be of a higher caliber. Traveling by motorcoach is a good way to go if you do not want to drive and if you like having someone else take charge of where you stop and what you see. Motorcoaches are more luxurious now than in the past.

Cons. Commercial buses tend to be crowded and uncomfortable. The worst part of commercial bus travel is that you have little or no control over where you sit or who sits near you. If the person in back of you is ill, drunk, or obnoxious, you might have to get used to it. In buses, often the windows are sealed shut, which results in stale air. This is not a good way to travel if you are prone to carsickness. Also, bus travel over long distances adds hours to your trip because of frequent stops.

Top 10 Reasons to Travel by Motorcoach

1. They do the driving.
2. You can see the scenery.
3. Sleep if you'd like.
4. Socialize with friends.
5. Enjoy a movie.
6. Most economical way to travel.
7. Door-to-door service.
8. Best for the environment.
9. Safer than driving yourself.
10. New, improved, luxurious.

Adapted from United Motorcoach Assn.

Train Travel

Pros. In America, train travel pales in comparison with that in other parts of the world, where trains are luxurious, efficient, and fast. Statistically, trains are one of the safest ways to travel in terms of accidents. At this writing, terrorist activity has not become an issue on trains, but Amtrak has added some new security procedures nevertheless. Like buses, trains are relatively inexpensive. Train travel is great for children because they can freely move around. Amtrak has jumped through hoops to make rail travel wheelchair accessible, which makes this a good option if you or your companion is disabled. The best train routes in the United States are on the East Coast, and on the West Coast from Seattle to Portland and Los Angeles to San Diego.

Cons. In Europe, trains are the desired mode of transportation. Here in America, the opposite is nearly true. Time, of course, is a major disadvantage of U.S. train travel. In the United States, choices of routes are limited. Amtrak does not get financing the way railways do in other countries, and therefore it has suffered tremendously in the last few decades. At press time, Amtrak had instituted an updated carry-on baggage policy with some new restrictions, but they were not checking all bags, which would require substantial financial investment. With the heightened possibility of domestic terrorism, I consider safety and security to be major concerns with train travel in the United States in the coming years, since this problem has not been sufficiently addressed.

> ### *Mary's Travel Gems*
>
> *Most people are surprised to learn that they can reserve their own private car on one of Amtrak's regularly scheduled departures and enjoy complete privacy and safety. Amtrak can even set up beverages and snacks in your private car. This is a great way to travel with large groups to a family reunion or on a business trip.* ✧✧✧

Air Travel

Pros. Air travel is still the safest way to travel long distances. Despite increasing delays, holdovers, and connection times, which are slated to get even longer in the next year or so, air travel is still quickest. Airline companies are trying to address the time-factor problem by introducing private entrances for preapproved travelers to accelerate check-in and security procedures. Most major hubs are already providing this option for celebrities, frequent business travelers, and airline club members. U.S. air carriers are required to provide accommodations for disabled people, which is a plus, although the hassles sometimes outweigh the advantages. If you can find specials, airfare is still a good value for travelers.

Some businesses that depend on air travel have found that chartering their own small planes is an excellent way to save time, money, and stress for their employees. These small planes avoid many of the hassles experienced by the ordinary passenger because they use their own private gates for arrival and departure.

Cons. Increased safety concerns are adding hours to air travel. No longer can you show up for a plane twenty minutes before departure and expect to get onboard. Also, the changing financial climate that began in 2001 has resulted in higher airfares and longer flight times as airline companies reroute to smaller airports to decrease congestion in the large hubs. Flying can be challenging with children and pets. I fly frequently out of necessity and choice, but I find airplanes to be mega-germ collectors. The air is recycled and the seat cushions and pillows are cleaned and disinfected almost never. Think about it: How often have you felt slightly sick after flying? The airline industry is starting to address some of these health concerns on behalf of disgruntled flight attendants, but they have a long way to go. Air travel is often cramped and uncomfortable. And do not even get me started on the food!

Cruise Travel

Pros. Hands down, cruise travel is the safest, healthiest, most comfortable way to travel for pleasure. The cruise ship is the floating hotel that takes you to multiple destinations. You sail by night and sightsee by day. Perhaps that is why cruise travel is the fastest growing area in the travel and tourism industry. Cruise ships are fun, educational, and safe. They are small countries, in fact, with their own government, infirmaries, and jails. They have lots of trained security personnel onboard, and the food is fabulous.

Are You a Cruiser?

There are two types of vacationers, the Resort Traveler and the Destination Traveler. The Resort Traveler is one who seeks sun, fun, sand, and surf. The Destination Traveler is one who seeks a more educational or cultural experience. If you're a little of both, cruising is a great option for you.

This is a terrific way to travel with children and people with special needs. The cabins are secure, comfortable, and luxurious. Like the airlines, cruise ships employ rigorous baggage and passenger screening. Cruise companies run special deals frequently, especially for groups and off-season or last-minute bookings.

Cons. Route flexibility and time are the biggest downsides to cruise travel. Cost might be another for you, but keep in mind that cruise travel includes room and board.

What or Who Will Need Attention While I Am Away?

Do you have pets you are leaving behind? Do you have plants, landscaping, or a pool that need maintenance? Which family members, friends, and neighbors should have a copy of your itinerary and important documents and paperwork? What about the safety and security of your home? Thievery and burglary spike during the summer months. The object of travel is to have a worry-free, safe, fun trip. Coming home to unpleasant surprises should not be part of that picture.

The Next Step

In my experience, I have found that 95 percent of all travel calamities would have been avoidable if the traveler had taken the time to do some thoughtful planning. Now that you have sketched out a rough draft of your trip's key elements, the next step is to actually *prepare* for your trip. Over the years, I have gathered hundreds of tried-and-true tips to make traveling safe, healthy, fun, educational, and totally rewarding. With the help of my insider secrets, you can too.

2
Making Travel Preparations
Planning a Safe and Healthy Trip

"If only . . ." If only I had thought to pack my prescription. If only I had taken the car for a check-up before we left. If only I had used travelers checks. Does this sound familiar?

I have my own long list of "if onlys"—major and minor travel calamities I could have avoided *if only* I had taken more time to prepare. Or to be fair to myself, *if only* I had known better. As you will discover, I have personally experienced just about everything that could go wrong on a trip, from car rental scams to thievery to shipjackings. These experiences have served me well. Thanks to my years as a travel industry insider and my vast travel experience, I have gained many learning opportunities that helped me acquire the tips and tricks I can now pass along.

Every bit of preparation and forethought that goes into your trip will save you countless "if onlys" later on.

Preparing Your Itinerary

If you went through the mental exercises I presented in the previous chapter, you are ready to get to work and make some nitty-gritty decisions about your trip. If you choose to do all of the research and planning yourself and want to make your own reservations, I can help you avoid some of the common traps. But first, let me try to steer you away from the book-it-yourself path.

Using a Travel Agent

The best way to save time, money, and headaches on your trip is to use a travel agent. Why do I say this? Because travel agents are travel professionals who have information at their fingertips. They know how to find the best deals. They keep up on the latest travel advisories. They can help you avoid long layovers, dicey connections, and unpleasant terminals. They are insiders who have experience with handling every kind of mishap imaginable. Most are specialists who know everything there is to know about your destination.

Thousands of travelers were stranded on September 11, 2001, unable to book flights home, find hotel rooms, rent cars, or arrange alternate transportation. Whom did they turn to? Travel agents. Travel agents responded immediately to the national crisis by securing reservations for their clients and rerouting them faster than anyone else.

I always use a travel agent, even though I know how to access many of their insider sources. I do this for two reasons: (1) My travel agent saves me time and money; and (2) My travel agent is better informed about up-to-the-minute developments, deals, and industry changes than I am. That is her job, and she does it exceptionally well.

Search Me

A new TSA ruling allows random airport security checks of your automobile. When entering airport property, authorities may search your automobile even if you never set foot in the terminal. Those who refuse the search have two options: leave the airport or turn around and park in an "off property" lot.

Do-it-yourself online booking and encyclopedic travel sites on the internet have made travel agents more competitive. To win new clients and hang on to old ones, travel agents now have to do their jobs better and offer more services than ever before. If you are still not convinced, see Chapter 5, "The New Millennium Travel Agent," to learn more about how a good travel agent can benefit you.

If safe, hassle-free, healthy, fun travel is your goal, step one is to use a travel agent when preparing your itinerary.

✈ MARY'S TOP TIPS FOR USING A TRAVEL AGENT

GET A REFERRAL OR RECOMMENDATION. Ask friends, relatives, and colleagues which travel agents they like, and why.

FIND AN AGENT WITH EXPERIENCE. Your travel agent should have a minimum of four years in the business. This is your gauge, just as it would be for your stock portfolio manager, for instance, or your insurance agent.

COME WITH A PLAN. Arrive with a plan and a budget. Tell your travel agent the purpose of your trip, where you want to go, how long you want to stay, whom you will be traveling with, and how much you want to spend. Offering definite parameters will help your travel agent make the best arrangements for you and your companions.

ASK A LOT OF QUESTIONS. Take advantage of the fact that your travel agent knows a great deal more about your destination and about travel in general than you do.

TAKE DUBIOUS NOTES. Log the name of the agent, date, and time in a notebook, and take down reservation and confirmation numbers. Keeping a careful paper trail helps you avoid misunderstandings later on.

If you and your travel agent discuss your trip in detail, you will have a more successful travel experience. Is this the cheapest fare, car rental, or room? If not, why not? Will my room be ready when I arrive? What kinds of hotel amenities can I expect? What will the weather be like? Is there anything unusual I should pack? What kinds of activities can I do while I am there? Are there special precautions I should take? What should I know

The Truth about e-Tickets

There is no difference, from a safety point of view, between paper tickets and e-tickets. As long as you have your printout with a confirmation number, the airline will honor your e-ticket. Airlines, in fact, have even begun to phase out paper tickets as a cost-cutting measure.

Internet at the Library

The public library is a woefully underused American institution these days. Most libraries now have computers and trained staff to help you find what you need on the internet. If you don't have a computer at home, research your upcoming trip at the library.

about the local customs? What is the best way to get around once I am there? Do I need travel insurance?

Your travel agent is a gold mine of information. You should get maps, travel advisories, sightseeing brochures, and tips galore—all included in the price of your trip.

Travel agents get commissions from hotels, resorts, tour operators, and cruise companies, but no longer from airlines. They now charge a booking fee that is anywhere from $25 to $35. From my point of view, this is a small price to pay for the time and money they save me, and for the information and resources they provide at no extra charge.

Booking Yourself

The Information Age is a wonderful thing. Anyone with time on their hands and access to a computer can research any kind of trip, from African safaris to barge travel along the canals of Europe. The amount of high-quality information you can find online about travel deals and destinations is limited only by your patience and energy for such pursuits.

If you want to book travel online, I recommend using sites that have a well-known track record. Stick with the ones you have heard of or that your friends recommend.

✈ Mary's Top Tips for Booking Travel Online

VERIFY CONTACT INFORMATION. Never use a website that does not have an address, phone number, and contact information. To avoid scams and potential problems, make sure there is a human being on the other end of your transaction who will be accountable.

CALL BEFORE YOU BOOK. Never make a reservation for a flight, cruise, hotel, or car without calling the online travel agent.

ASK IF YOU HAVE GOTTEN THE BEST DEAL. Some specials are not posted on the website. Write down the name of the person with whom you spoke, along with the time and date of that conversation.

DOUBLE-CHECK WITH THE COMPANY. After you find a car, hotel, cruise, or airline deal online, go directly to those companies via their website or toll-free number and ask if they can offer you a better price or if they have any special deals for those dates. Sometimes companies will give you an upgrade or offer you specials if you book through them directly. Ask what association discounts they offer. AAA and AARP memberships, for example, shave 10 percent off most rental cars and hotels.

GET A CONFIRMATION NUMBER. Never give your credit card information online until you have a confirmed reservation and a confirmation number. Print it out and put it with your other important documents. Have them mail you a travel voucher as backup.

B e wary of online bidding sites. I got stung by one of the popular travel auction houses for an airline ticket I purchased. Auction houses will not give you the time, route, or name of your flight until after you agree to purchase. I bid for—and got—a cheap ticket, which turned out to be on Delta Airlines. However, the flight date was a day later than the one I specified and would have been impossible for me to schedule. When I tried to cancel, the online bidding site refused. I informed them that passengers have the legal right to determine their own flight time. The company replied by saying that Delta had given them the rules. When I challenged them on this, which I knew to be untrue, and told them I was a travel industry insider, they hesitated, but didn't back down. I ended up eating that $179, even though I could have fought it successfully. It would have taken too much time and energy to fight.

Planning your arrival time. Most people who book their own flights overseas think they should plan it so they sleep on the plane and arrive bright and early the next morning. There are a couple of problems with this. First, you will be exhausted when you arrive, which means your antennas will be down and you will be an ideal target for opportunistic criminals. Second, your room will not be ready if you arrive much before noon. That could spell trouble.

I cannot tell you how many times I have seen jet-lagged tourists passed out in busy foreign hotel lobbies, their unattended bags heaped on the floor around them while they wait for their rooms to be ready. You can avoid this situation in several ways:

1. Book your overseas flight so you arrive after noon, when rooms are typically available.
2. Book your flight so you arrive in the evening and can soon go to sleep—the best cure for jet lag.
3. Contact the hotel ahead of time and find out if they can do an early check-in so you have a safe place to lock your bags and can take a quick catnap.

Planning for long layovers. Obviously, you will do your best to book connecting flights in such a way as to avoid long layovers. But what if you have no choice? Or what if your flight ends up getting delayed?

Assume that the worst could happen, and then prepare for it. Every airport has a website these days. You can find out ahead of time what your terminal offers in the way of amenities—everything from barbershops, places of worship, and museums, to business centers, duty-free shops, and children's play areas. Print out a map of the terminal and study it.

I was stuck in JFK Airport once for ten hours and—wouldn't you know—was horribly sick. I was absolutely miserable and couldn't wait to get on my flight. It was one of the longest ten hours I can remember. Only later did I learn that JFK has an infirmary. Had I known that, I could have seen a doctor, gotten medication, and been well on my way to recovery by the time I arrived home the next day.

Mary's Travel Gems

If your airport layover is going to be several hours, there is no reason to hang around the terminal, bored out of your gourd. Here are some of my favorite tips:
- Book a half-day room at an airport hotel and take a nap or watch a movie.
- Use the spa and workout room at an airport hotel.
- Reserve a taxi and go sightseeing in the city.   ✧ ✧ ✧

Airline member clubs are safe and wonderful places to relax. They offer comfortable chairs and couches, free local calls, clean bathrooms, and places to work that sometimes include internet modems, fax machines, and printers. Some offer free alcoholic beverages and complimentary food. If you are a frequent traveler and want to join one, do your homework to compare prices and benefits before you choose one airline club over another one. Some airlines let you join their clubs using frequent flyer miles. If you will be traveling with elderly companions or young children, consider a one-time pass, usually between $25 and $35, which you can purchase beforehand. This is a great way to add comfort to trips with long layovers.

For more tips on avoiding hassles in airports, see Chapter 3.

Travel insurance. If you are someone who likes to gamble, chances are you have never purchased traveler's insurance. News flash: The world of travel has changed. Unexpected flight delays are already becoming more commonplace because of heightened security measures and rerouting.

The chances of getting separated from your luggage or missing a connecting flight are now greater than ever. Terrorism, wars, and other unpredictable situations can spring up overnight. Enter travel insurance. A good insurance policy may reimburse you for lost luggage, medical evacuation, and travel delays, as well as accidental death.

One of the main reasons for travel insurance, however, is to protect your investment should something go wrong before or during your trip. It covers your contractual obligation to a cruise line, tour company, or vacation home or villa rental company and provides a refund of deposits you made if you or someone in your party had to cancel. Possible reasons might include illness, being called to jury or military duty, or suffering a catastrophe at home or in your business (such as a fire, getting laid off from a job, or being unable to leave work). Being the victim of an act of terrorism, unexpected quarantine, and getting caught in a natural disaster are other examples of events that could affect your travel plans and that your insurance might cover. I highly recommend that you look into travel insurance and *read the fine print carefully,* as each policy has exclusions and gotchas. "Acts of war," incidentally, are never covered.

E *ver since I had to jump ship in St. Lucia because my husband got very ill, I always buy travel insurance. It would have only cost me $35. Instead, I ended up using $3,000 out of pocket to leave the cruise and to pay for last-minute connecting flights home, taxis, hotel stays, and meals.*

Booking car rentals. I never, ever book rental cars on location. I always reserve them ahead of time. If you wait to secure a car when you arrive, you risk the possibility that the rental company will be fresh out of cars, or will not have the car you have budgeted for, or will only have cars that do not have the extras required for maximum safety and comfort. Always call your credit card company to find out how much car insurance they include. If you are going abroad, make sure your insurance is applicable in those countries as well.

✈ MARY'S TOP TIPS FOR RESERVING A CAR

PROTECT YOURSELF AGAINST GOTCHAS. If you are under 25, you could be slapped with an extra surcharge, or even barred from renting at all. Some companies will not let you pay with a debit card, personal check, or cash. Those that accept cash often require "cash prequalification," a process that could take several weeks. Check out the company website or ask the agent on the phone about these and other issues to avoid surprises later, such as mileage caps; daily versus weekend versus weekly rates; and penalties for returning the car early (or late).

BOOK WITH A KNOWN BRAND THAT IS ON AIRPORT PREMISES. Using an offsite mom-and-pop car rental company is asking for trouble. The national brands are almost always on the airport property or located very near with easy on/off access to the property, which means you do not have to drive miles away to some unknown part of town to pick up and return your car.

FIND A COMPANY THAT IS OPEN TWENTY-FOUR HOURS. I have been burned too many times by car rental companies that asked me to slip my keys into a drop-box at the end of my trip, and then sent me a bill for damage, extra miles, or other gotchas. You can avoid unexpected charges by speaking face-to-face with a representative at the end of your trip.

ASK FOR DISCOUNTS. Car rental companies, like hotels and airlines, offer specials and give discounts—but only if you ask. Find out if the rental company has partnerships with certain credit card companies or frequent flyer clubs.

For tips about what to do when you are ready to pick up your rental car, see Chapter 3.

Booking RV travel. What could be more fun than loading up family, friends, and pets and heading off on a road trip? RV travel combines the glamour of a rock-star road tour and the down-home fun of camping—without the bugs!

If you will be renting an RV overseas, your travel agent will have reams of information for you. RV travel in Europe is one of the fastest growing areas of the travel industry.

If you will be motorhoming domestically, your best bet is to check out the many resources and companies on the internet, as American travel agents are not fully equipped and experienced in this line of travel—yet. I have included some good RV rental resources in the Appendix.

The best way to have a safe and satisfying RV trip is to plan your itinerary thoroughly—and that includes mapping out your gas stops, food stops, sightseeing, route, and camping. RV rental companies offer road maps, camp locations, and information about places of interest along the way. Always consider the weather, especially if you will be traveling off-season. If you will be motorhoming in another country, do not forget to factor in its rainy season.

Which Car Models Are Safest?

When renting a car, is going small the best choice? Compare federal crash-test results for a particular car before you rent it by visiting www.nhtsa.dot.gov/cars/testing/ncap.

Quiz: Int'l Rainy Seasons?

Most of us forget about rainy seasons when planning a trip. Rain creates hazards on the road and can cause flight delays. How well can you match the countries, below, with their rainiest months?

  Vietnam
  Turkey
  Costa Rica
  Hawaii
  Japan
  Indonesia

  a. December–March
  b. October–March
  c. May–September
  d. November–March
  e. April–September
  f. May–October

Answers: c, b, f, d, e, a

Source: Travelleronline.com

✈ MARY'S TOP TIPS FOR RESERVING AN RV

SHOP AROUND. RV rental companies have become increasingly competitive. Call around before settling on one company.

CONSIDER THE FLY/DRIVE OPTION. Nothing can threaten your safety as much as driving home exhausted after a long vacation. RV rental companies offer terrific specials so the dangerous part of your trip (driving) can be a one-way proposition.

BEWARE OF THE "SARDINES IN A CAN" FACTOR. When looking into RVs, be wary of small units that claim to sleep five, six, or more. Ask for the measurement of the beds—adults need a full 6-feet length for comfort.

KNOW YOUR TERMINOLOGY. Do you know the difference between a motorhome, a mini-motorhome, and a travel trailer? Make a list of the features you absolutely cannot live without, such as self-contained kitchens and bathrooms, and then do your homework. Factor in your driving ability, though, when considering size. The Recreational Vehicle Rental Association has a helpful glossary of terms at its website (www.rvra.org).

TRAVEL OFF-SEASON. The rates for RV rentals go way down after the peak summer months. Consider a spring or fall trip. The highways and camping grounds will be much less crowded then as well.

To find out what to look for when you go to rent an RV, see Chapter 3.

Preparing for a Road Trip

For any kind of road travel, whether in your own car, a rental, or an RV, I highly recommend that you check out and join the Automobile Association of America (AAA). AAA is the grand-daddy of road-travel experts, and now has an informative website (www.aaa.com). On it and through them, you can get directions, tour books, TripTiks, order travel brochures, maps, and get traffic reports.

As I mentioned previously, driving is the most dangerous way to take a trip. You can decrease your chances of accidents and road mishaps by making some thoughtful preparations.

Downside of a Topside Carrier

- Can decrease fuel economy by as much as 10%.

- May prevent you from driving on certain parkways. In NY, e.g., the maximum vehicle height is 94 inches.

- Makes vehicle less stable in quick turns.

- May cause you to exceed your vehicle's total weight capacity (people plus cargo).

Source: AAA.com

I never, ever drive without my cell phone, even for short distances, and I always bring along the charger that plugs into the cigarette lighter. Recently, I was traveling across town when my radiator blew. It was beginning to get dark, I was in an unfamiliar area of town, and cars were rushing by me without stopping, even with my hazard lights blinking. Fortunately, I had thought to bring my cell phone. My phone didn't work inside my car, so I got out and raised it over my head, rotating in all directions, until I got a signal. The helpful person at AAA told me to get back in my car, lock the doors, turn off my hazard lights, and wait. Thankfully, the tow truck arrived within the hour, but by then it was pitch black. Thank goodness for cell phones!

Road Trip Checklist

☑ Inspect drive belts, which operate the air conditioner, power steering, and engine water pump.

☑ Check engine's cooling system.

☑ Freshen transmission fluid.

☑ Check battery.

☑ Inflate tires to ideal pressure.

☑ Organize document packet with registration, title, car manual, and emergency phone numbers.

☑ Pack a tool kit that contains: flashlight with fresh batteries; bungee cords; jumper cables; multi-tool; tire-changing wrench and jack; folding shovel; roll of duct tape; empty gas can; flares or reflective warning triangles; work gloves; and for winter, kitty litter for traction, ice scraper, and spray windshield de-icer.

☑ Pack a survival kit that includes: energy bars; water; prepaid calling card; first-aid kit; disposable camera to document accidents or crimes; notepad and pencil; whistle; rain poncho; blanket; moist towelettes; backpack; hat; and walking shoes.

☑ Invest in a good back pillow and high-quality sunglasses.

Making Health Preparations

Staying healthy while traveling anywhere in the world is always a challenge, but there are certain things we can do to protect ourselves and our family against illness and diseases. Please see the Appendix, where I have listed several important organizations that offer pre-travel advice, post-travel evaluation of health problems, and treatment for tropical diseases or other medical problems. There, I have also included emergency numbers and organizations that can offer medical help while you are traveling at home or abroad.

Your journey is a good occasion to remind yourself to keep your routine immunizations updated. About 80 percent of adults in the Western world have not maintained their immunization status since their school years. The immunization recommendations below are from the International Association for Medical Assistance to Travellers (IAMAT). IAMAT's list is intended as a general guideline. Your own immunization requirements depend on your individual health status, previous immunizations received, and your travel itinerary.

IAMAT recommends the following vaccinations before leaving the United States: tetanus-diphtheria; polio; measles-mumps-rubella; influenza; pneumococcal; and hepatitis A. Seek further advice from your physician or travel medical clinic.

Germ Alert

When the maintenance crews come onboard to clean the airplane, guess what never gets cleaned? The seat cushions and headrests. If seats could talk, you would be horrified to know what has been on that fabric. Put a pillowcase in your carry-on bag to rest your head against or to wrap the airline pillow in. Some people even buy teddy bears to use as pillows and give them away to a child upon arrival.

✈ Mary's Top Tips for Health Preparedness

FIND OUT WHAT VACCINATIONS OR MEDICATIONS ARE RECOMMENDED FOR YOUR DESTINATION COUNTRY. Every country is different, so be sure to use the resources in the Appendix to get the most recent information, and then verify that information with your physician.

MAKE SURE YOUR IMMUNIZATIONS ARE UP TO DATE. Those shots you had in your youth may no longer be protective.

HAVE OR BUY HEALTH INSURANCE. Call your HMO or health-insurance provider and find out exactly what they will cover abroad. Traveler's insurance is a great way to go, also.

GET THE NAMES AND ADDRESSES OF ENGLISH-SPEAKING DOCTORS. Your travel agent or insurance company can get these for you in advance.

GET A COPY OF YOUR CURRENT PRESCRIPTIONS. These would be necessary and helpful to a foreign physician unfamiliar with your health conditions.

IF YOU HAVE A MEDICAL CONDITION, MAKE ARRANGEMENTS TO HAVE YOUR OWN BLOOD. Or you can bring it with you on ice. Talk to your physician about the best and safest options.

GET A BROAD-SPECTRUM ANTIBIOTIC TO TAKE WITH YOU. Ask your doctor to write you a script for an antibiotic that is effective on upper respiratory as well as gastrointestinal bacteria.

KNOW WHERE TO GO FOR HELP. If you will be traveling to several cities or countries, get the names, addresses, and phone numbers of local physicians and hospitals.

MAKE A LIST OF MEDICATIONS YOU ARE ALLERGIC TO. In an emergency, you and your caregiver would have all the information on hand.

Protecting Your Pets, Possessions, and Home

An essential prerequisite for enjoying your trip is not having to worry about everything you left behind. This includes your home and the possessions in it, your lawn and pool, your pets, and your relatives. There is nothing worse when you are far from home than remembering that you forgot to turn something off or failed to cancel an appointment. Take preventive measures before you leave home so you can have peace of mind once you are far away.

> ### Don't Alarm Your Cat
>
> If you have an indoor/outdoor cat who comes and goes freely through a cat door, know that cats can set off the sensor alarm on many home security systems. If you are thinking of buying such a system for your home, inquire first about its sensitivity to pets.

Pre-trip Checklist

- ☑ Make a list of important phone numbers: friends, family, and neighbors; key business associates; contact information where you will be; personal physicians and dentists; lawyers; pet sitters and maintenance people. Leave one copy at home, one copy with a trusted neighbor, and bring one copy with you.
- ☑ Give itinerary with exact dates, credit card emergency numbers, traveler's insurance number, color copy of your passport, and hotel addresses, fax number, and emails to the same trusted person.
- ☑ Notify police and neighborhood watch associations that you will be gone, and ask them to check your house.
- ☑ Inform the post office and newspaper delivery service about your travel dates.
- ☑ Give a trusted neighbor a copy of your house key, and ask him or her to check your house and property while you are away.

- ☑ Get a timer on your house lights, and leave a car in the driveway if possible.
- ☑ Make arrangements for your pets and house plants.
- ☑ If you will be gone for an extended period, arrange for a neighbor or maintenance person to care for your lawn, garden, and/or pool.
- ☑ Turn off or unplug all unnecessary equipment.
- ☑ Turn down heat.

Packing for Your Trip

Now we come to one of my favorite topics: packing. I do a lot of seminars on land and onboard cruise ships, one of which is "The Joy of Packing." Half of the fun should be in planning and in getting there. The type of luggage you use and what you put in it greatly affect the success of any journey, and what you choose to take or leave behind can truly make or break your trip.

I always ask my audiences, "What is the very first thing to pack?" Their answers are quite revealing! I have heard everything from "makeup" to "my favorite family photos." Nope, I tell them. *The very first thing to pack is common sense, followed by a positive attitude, with your antennas in their upright position at all times.*

If you stop to think about everything that has gone wrong when you have traveled in the past, you would realize that most if not all of these sit-

---

Pack Your ACT

Attitude—put up your antenna; awareness is critical to safety.
Common sense—Use your street smarts and trust your basic instincts.
Tact—Diplomacy and kindness will take you a long, long way.

uations could have been avoided had you used common sense. When you are lost, overtired, stressed, or cranky, you become a target for crime and accidents. That is when you should pull out that common sense, also known as street smarts or basic instincts. And toting along a positive attitude will help you cope with inevitable unpleasant situations.

Your travel destination and the purpose of your trip will dictate everything about what you need to pack. Consider the following: (1) General climate and current weather; (2) Type of activities you will be doing; (3) How often you will need to dress up or down; (4) Local customs and etiquette.

Luggage

Luggage can either be your best friend or worst enemy. When it comes to luggage, you really do get what you pay for—so do not cheap out. There is nothing more aggravating than having a cheap luggage zipper split open mid-trip. When purchasing luggage, think of ease of movement when hopping on/off planes, boats, trains, ferries, and taxis.

Also, keep in mind that your luggage says a lot about you, just as your clothes do. Would you wear a mink coat on the streets of Washington, DC, at night? Would you wear flip-flops in the Vatican? Big, grubby backpacks bulging at the seams scream "Midnight Express!" in foreign countries. You will be searched. By the same token, ridiculously expensive luggage targets you for crime and extra scrutiny in airports. Use some common sense when choosing your travel gear.

Mary's Travel Gems

Before buying luggage, I try out different types and brands by carrying or rolling them between the store aisles to see how easily they maneuver, how comfortable the straps and handles are, and how well the wheels work. ❖❖❖

I *had a girlfriend who was traveling with me in Turkey and wanted to stay a few days longer, so she asked me if I would bring her large bag back to the States. It was a big favor, but I agreed— reluctantly. This piece of luggage was a high-end designer bag, very ostentatious. I had a bad feeling about going through customs. And sure enough, the agents stopped me and opened it up to see if I was smuggling expensive goods out of the country without paying the requisite duty. She also forgot to give me the pulley to snap on her bag to drag it, so I had to rent a trolley. Irksome!*

Keep in mind that new FAA security regulations limit airline passengers to one carry-on bag plus one personal item. Your carry-on must not exceed 45 linear inches (length + width + height) or weigh more than 40 pounds. Personal items are defined as: purse; briefcase; laptop; small book-bag style backpack; or small tote bag or shoulder bag that does not exceed 36 linear inches (length + width + height). Additional items that are allowed include: outer garments such as sweaters, coats, and hats; approved child safety seat for lap or ticketed child; umbrella stroller; diaper bag; reading material; bistro-sized or smaller bag of consumable food.

Cruise ships, trains, and buses have their own regulations, and baggage regulations also vary from airline to airline, so check with your travel company first to find out what they allow and disallow. *Be aware that the familiar policies of last year probably no longer apply.* For example, trains now only allow two pieces of luggage, no exceptions, at 50 pounds maximum. Avoid unpleasant surprises at check-in. Your travel agent would have all of this detailed information at her fingertips.

Unfortunately, baggage handlers here and abroad are notorious thieves. I've lost several valuable items packed inside my checked-through luggage. The last time it happened was on a trip to Greece. In a last-minute shopping spree in Athens, I found a fabulous Louis Vitton–style bag in the area called the Plaka, famous for its wonderful luggage shops specializing in high-end designer knock-offs. It was a bag I could use as a briefcase, definitely one-of-a-kind, and I just loved it. I threw it into my suitcase on the way to the airport. When I got back home, I thought I was going mad. I looked everywhere for my treasured purchase, but couldn't find it. Then I realized that a baggage handler must have unzipped my luggage, removed my new bag, rezipped my luggage, and sent it on its way. Since using a combination lock on all of my bags, I've never been ripped off. However, new regulations give baggage handlers the right to open our bags, even if they are locked!

The walking-talking suitcase. Want to know what my absolute favorite piece of luggage is? Me, wearing a multi-pocket travel vest! I would have to say, hands-down, that a travel vest is the most valuable piece of "luggage" you can invest in. You can purchase travel vests at any good camping outfitter. Mine is khaki-colored and has zippered, Velcro, buttoned, and flap pockets inside and out. I am never without a tissue or loose coins when I visit foreign toilets, nor am I ever without a small tube of sunscreen or lip balm. I hook my Swiss army knife onto a loop inside one pocket, and keep an energy bar in another. I always have sunglasses, maps, and my trusty cell phone. However, I keep my cash and cards and emergency numbers and documents next to my body, in a money belt. The point is, *with a travel vest, you can keep your hands free, and still have on your person everything you need for just about any situation.*

✈ Mary's Top Tips for Luggage

PACK A SMALL, EXPANDABLE BAG INSIDE YOUR MAIN BAG. Inevitably, you will get ready to pack for your return trip and realize you have more than you came with! Shopping is one of the great joys of travel, so be prepared.

PACK AN EMPTY DAY PACK OR MINI BACKPACK. For sightseeing, this is a necessity for holding personal items, water, and small purchases while leaving your hands free.

INVEST IN LUGGAGE STRAPS AND PLASTIC TIES FOR CARRY-ON, AND PACK A COMBINATION LOCK. New TSA regulations allow luggage handlers to open your carry-on bags without your permission. Use straps around your carry-on luggage, and secure baggage with plastic lock ties—the type used to secure jumbo garbage bags. If handlers need to open your bag, they will not have to break an expensive lock. Pack a combination lock inside your luggage to use for locking up your valuables *in your hotel room.*

NEVER PUT YOUR HOME ADDRESS OR PHONE NUMBER ON YOUR BAG. If you do, you are asking for all kinds of trouble. I use my own name but a post office box address. A business address works well too.

Packing Tips

Think small and light. Get a calendar and mark each day of your trip according to what you visualize you will be doing. Include the first day and the last day—your travel days. Stand in front of your bed (make sure it has nothing on it) and lay out your clothes day by day. Include all of your accessories, shoes, bags, and work-related as well as personal items. Now you can begin the process of organizing.

✈ MARY'S TOP TIPS FOR CHECK-THROUGH PACKING

CHOOSE CLOTHES THAT WILL MIX AND MATCH. Navy/tan and black/tan are all-around good colors. The more versatile your clothing, the less you will have to lug around. Plain clothing that you can accessorize with a scarf, vest, or belt work best.

THINK CONSERVATIVELY. Americans tend to be surprised by the fact that in other cultures, especially cosmopolitan European cities, conservative attire is preferred, particularly for tourists. Leave short shorts, miniskirts, revealing clothing, and loud, obnoxious tee shirts at home.

CHOOSE FABRIC THAT IS VERSATILE. Cotton and microfibers are good travel choices, since they are comfortable, washable, and breathe easily. You may not be able to shower as often on your trip as you do at home.

CHOOSE YOUR SHOES WISELY. Most Americans run out and buy new designer white sneakers—a big mistake, since it marks you as a target. Instead, buy comfortable walking shoes. I recommend soft walking or hiking shoes (not boots). Choose beige, tan, or grey colors that blend in well with the local styles of the culture.

BRING AT LEAST TWO ZIPPER-LOCK PLASTIC BAGS, DIFFERENT SIZES. You will be glad you did when your necklace breaks apart, your vitamin bottle gets crushed, or your socks get wet.

PACK AN EXPANDABLE NYLON BAG. You can use it as a shopping bag, a laundry bag, or to carry extra or breakable purchases.

PACK BUBBLE WRAP AND TAPE. If you purchase a fragile item, you can protect it on the trip home.

Carry-on packing. Carry-on packing is an art in itself. If you think all you need for a two-hour bus, train, or airline trip is a good book, think again. Expect the worst—that you could be separated from your checked-through luggage—and then prepare for it. You should have on your person everything you absolutely need. Here is a checklist to help you.

Carry-on Checklist

- ☑ Documents: money, travelers checks, credit cards, passport, visa, and important phone numbers and information
- ☑ Pillowcase, to cover your headrest and airline pillow
- ☑ Self-addressed, stamped padded mailer. If security wants to remove a treasured comb, manicure set, or knitting needles from your carry-on bag, you can mail an item back to yourself right at the airport instead of saying good-bye to it forever.
- ☑ Contact lens case, eyeglasses, and essential toiletries. The airlines will give you a courtesy bag of essentials with items such as a toothbrush and tooth-paste if they lose your check-through luggage. But if there are personal-care items you cannot part with, bring them with you in your carry-on bag.
- ☑ Four days of prescription medicine, and any medical accessories. If you are currently taking medication or depend on a device such as an inhaler, bring it with you—enough for at least four days. Have your doctor mail you written prescriptions ahead of time, and bring them with you.
- ☑ Bottled water and food. Hydrating is one of the best ways to fend off illness and travel fatigue. Always bring healthy snacks with you, as well, in case you get trapped on an airplane or in a traffic jam or find yourself in an emergency situation in which you are not free to leave.

☑ Band-Aid, antibacterial cream, and moist towelettes. If you get a cut, take care of it immediately. When you travel, you will be exposed to super-bacteria from around the world, new strains of which can kill within twenty-four hours.

Carrying your valuables. The American dollar is accepted anywhere. You should have about $50 in cash on you, no more. However, it is always a good idea to get that amount in the local currency to cover taxicabs, a beverage, or an unexpected fee at your destination.

Carrying a purse is a recipe for disaster. I keep my money and important documents in a money belt next to my skin, under a loose-fitting shirt. Wherever I go, it goes. Fanny packs are great for small items such as a comb, lipstick, and towelettes, but never keep money or valuables in them. I am also a big fan of travel vests—heavy-duty cotton vests with a gazillion pockets that you can buy through the mail from camping and adventure-gear vendors such as Eddie Bauer or Banana Republic. Mine allows me to bring along everything I need and still keep my hands free.

Before You Leave for a Foreign Country

Language. Even for travel pros like myself, there are always surprises waiting in a foreign land—and that is part of the appeal. The first one, of course, is the language. Do yourself and every American a favor: Buy a phrase book in the language of the country you will be visiting. If you attempt to communicate in the native tongue, chances are the person with whom you are speaking will answer you in perfect English! If you do not even try, you can expect much worse treatment.

Here are six phrases or terms you absolutely must master:

1. *How much...?*
2. *Where is...?*
3. *Hello.*
4. *Thank you.*
5. *Toilet.* Do not say restroom, do not say ladies' or men's room or washroom or water closet. The word *toilet* is international. When you need to find one, ask for one.
6. *Police.* The word *police* is another international word. Scream it if you need to. If you yell "Help!" you may not get it.

> ### Travel Gadgets and Essentials
>
> Here are some things to pack that you might not think about:
>
> - Swiss army knife with scissors, cork screw, and screwdrivers for cutting cheese and opening bottles and cans
> - Mini-flashlight
> - Hot water heater and travel tea or coffee bags
> - Travel-size tissue pack

Local customs. There is no excuse these days for being an Ugly American. There are countless travel guides out there in bookstores, at libraries, and on the internet jam-packed with valuable information about the culture you are getting ready to experience. For successful travel, you will need to know about the climate, health advisories, and political advisories. But equally important for your safety and health are the local customs. Find out about such things as tipping etiquette, accepted behavior, and gender-related expectations. Remember: You will not be home, so do not expect your destination to be like home. That is the best advice I can give anyone getting ready to embark on a foreign adventure.

Cell phones. For the ultimate sense of safety and security, rent a cell phone with international cellular service for your overseas trip. You will save money on local and overseas phone calls, and your family will have an easy way to reach you as well. It is a great way to make reservations for dinner, theatre, or concerts, too. The cellular service company will program in the cell towers for the countries you will be visiting, and provide you with all of the emergency numbers for those areas. Best of all, it is unbelievably inexpensive.

Currency and credit cards. People ask me all the time, what kind of currency is best for overseas travel? Here is what I recommend you bring.

Money Checklist

- ☑ <u>Two credit cards.</u> MasterCard and Visa are accepted virtually everywhere. Always bring both, because there are places, such as car rental companies, that require two credit cards for identification. Most vendors will assume if you have two cards in the same name, then they are probably legitimate.

- ☑ <u>An American Express card.</u> Why do I say this, when so many establishments do not accept it? Because American Express automatically insures for theft. Use your American Express card, if you can, for expensive purchases.

- ☑ <u>$50 in the local currency.</u> You can change money at your destination airport, but I recommend doing it here in the States. You will get a better exchange rate, and you will not have to contend with the long, long lines that form as soon as your plane lands.

- ☑ <u>Good old green.</u> American money is loved everywhere. It never hurts to have a few dollars to use in taxis, in restaurants, in train terminals, and in the airport.

☑ <u>Travelers checks.</u> Travelers checks are safe, as long as you keep the receipts separate from the checks. Always leave one copy in your suitcase and one at home. Some businesses—taxicabs, for example—do not accept travelers checks, which is why a small amount of currency is essential.

Ready, Set, Go

Now you can leave for your trip knowing that you have done everything possible to prepare for a successful travel experience. Lots of things can still go wrong on your trip, however, which I will tell you about in the next chapter. Get ready for an adventure!

3

In Transit

What Could Go Wrong and How to Prevent It

I always tell people that travel is accelerated living—you get maximum thrills per minute. When you go on a trip, you are exchanging dollars for experiences. Making the most of those experiences is what this book is all about. However, even with the best-laid plans, you should still expect the unexpected. Lots can happen to you in transit. Cars break down, planes get delayed, the weather can turn bad—situations you cannot avoid. But there are plenty of precautions you can take to avoid the avoidable once you have left home, and plenty you can do to survive the unexpected. Let's start with land travel.

Renting a Car

Because you booked your rental car in advance, there should be a car reserved and waiting for you when you arrive at the car rental company. But that does not mean you are ready to drive away. There is still the matter of inspecting your car, reading the fine print, verifying your rates, and signing the papers.

If you heeded my advice from the previous chapter, you also took the time to review your home auto insurance policy as well as the coverage offered by your credit cards to see if they cover rental car liability and collision. It is better to know ahead of time what you are covered for in the

The cost of renting a car in Europe can be as much as 40 percent higher than renting in the States. Add to that the higher cost of gasoline, highway tolls, and taxes of 17 percent or more, and it can be an expensive proposition.

event of an accident, because car rental agents can be very persuasive in trying to get you to purchase additional insurance. Why spend extra bucks on duplicate coverage?

There is nothing quite as annoying as getting a surprise at the end of your trip in the form of add-ons and extras on your car rental bill. If you cannot name exactly how much the car will cost at the time you return it—to the last penny—then you have not done your job as a careful consumer.

In European countries, such as the Czech Republic, Albania, Poland, Hungary, Italy, and Turkey, rental car theft is rampant. In fact, your credit card insurance may not even cover theft in these countries. Most theft insurance does not apply on a ferry or in the Chunnel, either. Read the fine print and ask questions before you rent a car abroad so you do not get in trouble later.

Here are some other ways to avoid problems with your rental car.

✈ MARY'S TOP TIPS FOR RENTING A CAR

JOIN A FREQUENT TRAVELER'S PROGRAM. These give you great discounts, upgrades, and other perks, such as bypassing long lines. Some companies let you join on the spot.

BRING YOUR CONFIRMATION NUMBER WITH YOU. This will bring up the time and date of your reservation on their computer, so there should be no question of availability, model type, and locked-in rate.

BRING CREDIT CARDS. Few car rental companies accept cash on the spot. Some accept cash if you have prequalified to pay this way. Many foreign countries require two major credit cards as ID.

ALWAYS INSURE YOUR COMPANION AS AN ADDITIONAL DRIVER. Even if you plan to drive the entire way, circumstances such as illness could necessitate another driver, and then you would be liable if your companion got into an accident.

EXAMINE THE CAR THOROUGHLY, INSIDE AND OUT. Check for scratches, dents, torn upholstery, broken lights, stains—you name it. Check all instruments, including brakes, wipers, radio, blinkers, and lights. Take notes. Report your findings to the agent and keep a written record.

REVIEW YOUR RATES BEFORE YOU SIGN ANYTHING. Questions you should ask include: What will I be charged if I return the car several hours late? Would it be cheaper to rent by the week and return the car earlier than it would be to rent by the day or by the weekend? Are there any hidden costs, taxes, or add-ons I should know about? Ask for a printout of your bill.

VERIFY THAT THE RETURN LOCATION WILL BE OPEN WHEN YOU RETURN THE CAR. As I have mentioned before, key-drop boxes are an invitation for future disputes about mysterious or unwarranted charges.

INQUIRE ABOUT A NAVIGATIONAL SYSTEM. Many rentals come equipped with a Global Positioning System (GPS). If yours does not, find out how much it would cost to get one. This is a wonderful tool for finding your way, especially in unfamiliar cities.

ASK FOR AN EXTRA KEY. Some rental companies will provide you with a spare key, free of charge.

RENT A CELL PHONE. Never, ever take a road trip without one. Walkie-talkies are also great, especially when traveling with kids.

BRING WINDOW SCREENS FOR BACKSEAT PASSENGERS. Makeshift sun blockers such as pillowcases and newspapers rolled up in the window are hazardous for driving, so come prepared on long trips.

Before you drive off, familiarize yourself with the car's controls. "Play" with the radio, adjust the mirrors, and turn on the lights and wipers. Get to know your "new" car.

Getting lost is the perfect way to get into trouble. Avoid this by reviewing your maps before you set off, and have them in a handy place.

O n a business trip in Alaska, I rented a car and figured I had plenty of time to make it to my business meeting. I was in for a surprise. They weren't about to let me go anywhere just yet. Because of frigid temperatures and the danger of sudden inclement weather, Alaskan rental car dealers make you practice an emergency survival drill. I was issued a full-body, Day-Glo-orange warm-up suit, and told to put it on. They showed me how to make the heaters work and this, that, and the other. I looked like a psychedelic snowman. They warned me to never, ever leave my car in the event of a breakdown. Oh, yes, and they warned me not to talk to the bears!

Renting an RV

Renting an RV is similar to renting a car, but more involved. To protect your safety and pocketbook, go through all of the same preparations and take the same precautions as I have mentioned above. However, a recreational vehicle, depending on the type you get, requires a level of mastery that simple driving does not. You will have to learn how to use the water system, appliances, and generator, for example. You will also need to know the proper way to maneuver in tight spots, lock up at night, and gas up.

In addition to taking copious notes, I recommend using a video recorder or even a simple tape recorder while the dealer demonstrates and explains the various functions. Ask a lot of questions. Practice, with the dealer watching you. Obviously, you should ask the dealer to check every piece of equipment onboard before you go on your merry way to verify that the RV is in tip-top shape. Otherwise, you will be liable for repairs later on.

Safety and Security on the Road

Okay. So you have your emergency tools with you, water and snacks in case you get stranded, blankets, good shoes, first-aid kit, and maps galore. You are super ready for a fabulous road trip. Nothing could go wrong, right?

Wrong! Allow me to play devil's advocate for a moment, because the only thing in life that is certain is *uncertainty*.

What to Do If You Get Lost

I love to get lost when I am wandering around in a foreign city. But driving is another matter. It is not fun to be driving on the thruway in the wrong direction and have no clue when the next opportunity to turn around will be coming up. If you do not have a navigational system built into your car, the next best thing is to stop for directions.

Here, as in most other cases, common sense is your best ally. Particularly at night, in a strange city, do not slow down the car and flag over the nearest passerby, no matter how panicked you feel. Instead, take the time to find a populated, well-lit place such as an all-night convenience store or gas station to stop and ask. If you are traveling

Broken Lighters

When you rent a vehicle, make certain the cigarette lighter works. You will need a working lighter to recharge your cell phone, which you should never be without on the road.

More RV Tips

- To minimize backing up problems, experienced RVers find "pull through" camping sites and large shopping center parking lots in town.
- When backing up is necessary, always station a companion behind the RV to guide you.
- Always use the slow lane.
- Avoid driving at night.
- Go through a checklist every time you depart for a new destination:
    - Is the step retracted?
    - Are the doors locked?
    - Are all loose items inside secured?
- Try to accelerate smoothly and anticipate sudden stops so you can bring the unit to a halt smoothly.

alone, do not announce in a loud voice that you are lost. Consider phrasing your question like, "What is the best way to get to...?"

Road Rage

People get nuts behind the wheel. If someone tailgates you because you are driving too slowly, or flips you the bird because you accidentally cut him off, I have two words of advice for you: *Don't engage.* Forget making the peace sign, honking back, or getting revenge with passive-aggressive driving techniques. These days, you are better off with a help-less shrug, a kind smile, and then nothing else. Look away and withdraw your energy.

D *riving along on the thruway last summer, I became aware that my windshield, coated with dust, dead bugs, and some kind of pollen that was in the air, was making it hard for me to see well in the bright sun. I spritzed the windshield about ten times with my wipers on high speed until the glass was clear. Suddenly, from out of nowhere, a large biker in black leather with skulls on his storm trooper helmet appeared within arm's reach of my driver-side window. He was yelling a vulgarity at me, punctuated by a certain hand gesture. Mind you, we were racing along at 70 or so. I was so stunned that I merely mouthed "Sorry" and shrugged with a quizzical look. He scowled, cursed a few more times to make sure I got the message, and then gunned it to 90 and disappeared. He was a mere speck on the horizon before I realized what had happened. My wiper fluid must have flown back into his face—a life threatening condition for a motorcyclist. A good thing to remember next time a Hell's Angel is motoring behind you.*

Breakdowns

You remembered to bring your cell phone, right? If your car breaks down, the first thing to do is pull over, put on your hazard lights, and call your automobile club or a towing company.

Next, get back in your car and turn off the hazard lights. Lock the doors and wait. Nothing shouts *victim* as loudly as a single person or a helpless couple standing beside the road wishing for a kind volunteer to pull over and help. If someone does stop and offer to help, politely tell that person that there is a tow truck on the way, but remain in your vehicle.

Not so easily done in a foreign country, although AAA is an international organization. I have used it in London and Paris, for example. But if you are deep in the countryside, far from urban areas, you might have to rely on the kindness of strangers.

Pull Off—Way Off

Studies have shown that cars parked on the shoulder are often struck by passing traffic, especially at night. Pull well off the highway if you break down, even if you have a flat tire and think you should not drive, and wait for help to arrive. Do not take a nap and do not leave your car.

F riends of mine who used to work for the airlines always kept a stash of Playboy *magazines and small airline bottles of liquor with them when they drove through Mexico. In case of roadside problems, little gifts, they said, always seemed to go a long way.*

Money always works too. Have on you enough cash that you can get yourself out of a jam when you are driving in a foreign country.

Accidents

There are no two ways about it: Driving is dangerous. The best ways to avoid traffic accidents are to take your time, drive defensively, and stay alert and awake.

Most people do not realize that in foreign countries when you have an accident, they expect you to pay on the spot if it is a minor incident. I always carry some local currency and American dollars for such emergencies when I drive in Europe. I shudder to think about all of the sheep, goats, chickens, and shepherds I have narrowly avoided hitting.

I n a remote part of Turkey, I had a minor accident and had to wait for a policeman to show up. He demanded a million something in lira, which really isn't a lot of money over there, and took me off the side of the road out of view to give me my ticket. I'm too old to be sold for white slavery, but I nevertheless conjured up images of the movie Midnight Express—getting busted for some drug he'd plant on me that I've never heard of. Fortunately, I fumbled around in my purse until I produced the necessary cash to pay him off. There was an awkward moment when I didn't know if that would be enough to appease him. Then he saw my California driver's license and started pointing and saying, "Mickey Mouse! Mickey Mouse!" I nodded and smiled enthusiastically and played along until the tension broke and he let me go back to my car.

Rest and Gas Stops

Rest stops scare me to death. Unless it is an absolute emergency, do not pull into a rest stop that appears to be empty. Drive the few extra miles until you come to one with food and gas vendors. Even populated rest stops are havens for petty thieves, however. Always lock you car. Beware of rest stop bathrooms. Make certain that you keep your purse or briefcase near you, and do not set anything on the restroom floor where a watchful snatcher can grab it from under the stall.

In Europe, gas stations are self-pump and very intimidating. Only in America do we have gas station attendants. Read your guide books well, because figuring out how to use the pumps and how to convert to liters and use local currency is difficult, even for seasoned travelers like me. Travel guides offer helpful tips about country customs and procedures.

Crossing Borders and Checkpoints

I have driven in some pretty dicey places. When crossing into another country, expect to be stopped and questioned. Do not act impatient or you will pay the consequences. The best rule of thumb when confronted with security people is to smile, be pleasant, and cooperate. Above all, use common sense. Know the border rules before setting off. Do not have anything in your vehicle that could be considered illegal, improper, or suspect.

Crossing into Canada. Many Americans, for instance, do not know that they need special documents when driving from the United States into Canada. For a short-term visit to Canada, you will need a valid passport, unless you are an American citizen or permanent resident arriving from the States, in which case you must provide proof of citizenship or residency upon request. Proof of citizenship consists of a passport, original or certified copy of your U.S. birth certificate, current voter's registration card, U.S. military discharge papers, or certificate of citizenship or naturalization. If you are a permanent resident of the United Stated, but not a U.S. citizen, you must provide your "green card" if requested. Persons under eighteen years traveling without parents should have a letter of authorization from a parent or guardian to travel into Canada.

Crossing into Mexico. You will need the same documents as above for traveling to Mexico. In addition, you will need to present a Tourist Card, without which you will not be allowed to enter Mexico. You can obtain a Tourist Card from any airline office servicing Mexico or from the Mexican consulate. You must also present a photo ID, such as a valid driver's license.

Buses and Trains

Compared with driving yourself, buses and trains are fairly safe. Yet unpleasant or dangerous incidents still occur.

I was traveling on a train through Italy to Switzerland doing research for one of my seminars called "Traveling Single in a Doubles World." The trains in Europe have first-class compartments that accommodate several passengers, and there were four others in mine. As it was getting dark, I decided to go to the dining car for dinner and a drink. In a passageway, I met a man in his early twenties who began talking to me. He was from New York and we struck up a conversation. After dinner, I was walking back to my compartment when this man appeared again. He pushed me against a wall and started to sexually assault me. With an incredible rush of adrenaline, I pushed and screamed, but there was no one around. Managing to break free, I ran back to my compartment. When I got there, the other passengers were gone, and this man followed me into the car and harassed me for the next three hours to Switzerland. He got my name and address off my bag (that was the last time I ever put my own address on my ID tag) and *threatened to find me in Oregon. What could I have done differently? I should have run straight to the conductor instead of returning to my car.*

In Europe, train terminals are the heartbeat of the city—thriving, bustling centers of commerce and culture. Not so in America, where train stations are sometimes not well maintained and become refuges for homeless people. Rule number one, whether you are at a train or a bus terminal: Do not part company with your bag. Professional thieves live and lurk in train and bus terminals, and they will find a way to cause a nearby commotion and distract you if they observe that your purse or briefcase is sitting on the floor unwatched. While your attentions are focused elsewhere, a member of their team will pluck your bag and it will be gone in a flash before you know what hit you.

On buses, except for charters, the major problems you will confront are unsavory passengers. What do you do if you end up in a seat next to someone who is obnoxious, drunk, or possibly dangerous? Tell the driver. The driver may be able to arrange for you to move to a different seat. He is also in radio contact with higher ups, who may wish to have the passenger removed at the next stop. On trains, go to the conductor. Although sparse, trains do have security personnel aboard. A second solution is to get the community involved. Talk to others around you and see if they can help.

O *ne problem I've encountered several times on buses where I was tour director is bad driving. I've had to move up to the seat behind the driver and say, "Excuse me, but you seem to be falling asleep and not paying attention." On one such trip in Hawaii, the driver was actually watching sumo wrestling on a small TV mounted next to his rear-view mirror the whole time he was driving! It was both horrifying and maddening, but I'm sure that's how he came to think of me. I bugged him the entire trip.*

At national borders, buses are stopped and all of your bags will be thrown onto the ground so you can go through customs. Keep your eye on your luggage at all times and get to it as soon as possible.

Regarding both trains and buses, never leave anything valuable in your seat when you go to the lavatory. I keep my money belt next to my skin, under my shirt, even when I go to the bathroom. Leaving a purse in your seat is an invitation for trouble.

Air Travel

Air travel has actually gotten safer since September 11. But we live in unpredictable times. So start your trip with a relaxed but alert, positive attitude, and that will set the tone for everything that follows.

In the Airport

A tremendous amount of work and debate has been going on about airport security since the 2001 attacks on America. The government has given over an enormous amount of money, time, and training to federalize security personnel. However, I have not seen a significant change in the way bags and passengers are screened. I find security in American airports to be irregular, sometimes annoying, and not altogether effective. So, get those antennas up. If something were to happen, you would only have seconds to react.

Some of the new security technologies being tested right now in airports are: (1) Wireless handheld computers that allow state troopers patrolling terminals and parking garages to check a vehicle's license plate or criminal history, outstanding arrest warrants, and the immigration status of anyone they consider suspicious; (2) Computer software and closed-circuit cameras in airport passageways that match the faces of known terrorists and other criminals to travelers arriving and departing; (3) "Smart" alarm systems that can pinpoint a security breach inside a terminal to avoid needless evacuations of parked airplanes and entire terminals;

(4) High-capacity X-ray machines to detect bombs; and (5) Trace detectors, which look for microscopic quantities of explosives inside and outside a bag that are presumed to be present if it contains a bomb.

A word about film. Many people mistakenly believe X-ray machines that scan carry-on items will damage film and electronic media. That is false; the level of X-ray radiation is too low to cause damage. However, if that film is X-rayed, say, five times on a trip, you might see an effect called "X-ray fog," a haze over the image that cannot be corrected in the lab. It is no longer safe, however, to stow your film in your check-through luggage. The CT scanner and many of the high-energy X-ray systems now used to examine checked luggage can damage film (but not electronic media).

H ow great is the "new" security in American airports? I hate to be parted with my beloved Swiss Army knife when I travel, so I decided to try an experiment. I smuggled it inside my carry-on bag all the way through security from Seattle to Portland to Juneau, Alaska, and back—and it never got detected. (I had my self-addressed stamped Jiffy envelope with me in case it did.) Another day, I sat down and watched the security people for about half an hour at Seattle International Airport. What did I see? They were incredibly lax. They continued to drink their coffee and chitchat and be very nonchalant while observing the passengers. I watched the police too, also on their cell phones half of the time chatting. I was just amazed.

Like train and bus terminals, airports are havens for professional criminals. Because of the presence of security and density of the crowds, violent crime is not much of a problem in airports. But pickpockets, purse snatchers, and petty thieves are. Here are some measures you can take to minimize airport-related problems.

✈ Mary's Top Tips for Airport Safety

Leave for the airport with time to spare. Rushing is one of the best ways to forget something critical, let down your guard, or get into a mishap that could ruin your trip.

Arrive at the airport early. With increased security, expect to spend a lot of time at check-in and security. Give yourself an hour and a half cushion for domestic flights, two and a half hours for overseas flights.

Never part company with your bags. Not even for a moment. Keep small bags off the floor in bathroom stalls.

Be extra vigilant at the security gate. This is where computers disappear and purses vanish. Do not place your bag onto the conveyor belt until you have emptied your pockets and are ready to go through the metal detector.

If security singles you out, act pleasant and be patient. It is happening more and more that little old ladies and other nonthreatening types are being pulled aside and made to take off their shoes, submit to wand scanners, and open up handbags. If you are selected, stay cool.

Wait for your flight in a populated area. In airports, safety in numbers is the name of the game. Surveillance cameras are sometimes located in designated waiting areas at gates.

Report anyone or anything suspicious. Airport employees are trained to spot unusual behavior, but many eyes are better than a few. Look for people who seem nervous and edgy, and try to make eye contact with them. You can tell a lot by looking into someone's eyes.

In case of emergency, stay low and blend in. In the event of a skirmish, gunman, or hostage situation, make yourself invisible. Unlike airplanes, airports are swarming with ground security and they will arrive soon. In the airport terminal, being a hero could get you killed. On the airplane, it is another matter.

On the Plane

Being on an airplane is a bit like going to a restaurant. Good etiquette goes a long way toward making your flying experience a good one. Remember that flight attendants are service people. You will get better service by being polite. You will get better service if you are dressed nicely. And you will get better service if you do not smell. Reading the book *Plane Insanity,* by flight attendant Elliott Hester, reminded me of all the shocking behavior I have seen on planes, including the awful odors coming from fellow passengers. Be respectful of your close-quarter neighbors when you fly, and they will likely be respectful back.

Although planes are not generally considered safe havens for thieves, I have never wanted to test the possibility. That is why I always take my valuables to the lavatory with me. I keep my money belt under my shirt, and it goes where I go. The only possessions you should leave in your seat untended are items that you can replace.

Preventing illness. I mentioned it previously, but I will say it again: Airplanes are germ collectors. You do not want to know what your seat cushion and headrest have been through. Once you get situated on the plane, get out your pillowcase and put it behind your head. You may not be able to see the germs, but trust me, they are there. Just ask anyone in the industry how often the seats are laundered and you will never have the same casual attitude about those seats again.

Wash your hands frequently during your flight. I always keep moist towelettes or a small bottle of waterless hand-washing solution.

Drink lots of water, preferably your own. When I see a flight attendant reaching over my empty cup to get a can of soda or some ice, I politely pass on the airline beverage. Why? Because flight attendants are germ carriers too—they pick up germs from all over the globe and carry them onboard. They use their bare hands to handle both your food and your throwaways. And they spend hours on germ-infested airplanes.

If you get a paper cut or any kind of open wound on the plane, immediately wash it, put antibacterial cream on it, and cover it with a Band-Aid.

This simple precaution could literally save your life. Do not take the chance of contracting deadly, exotic bacteria.

Fear of flying. If flying makes you extremely nervous, sweaty, or even makes you cry, I recommend that you seek professional help. There are many effective ways to treat fear of flying. Even people who do not consider fear of flying a huge problem may experience some common symptoms such as rapid breathing, chest pain, increased heart rate, stomach discomfort, and mild anxiety. If this happens to you, do some controlled deep breathing or listen to some relaxing music if you are on a long flight equipped with passenger headsets. If your anxiety does not go away and is getting worse, do not be shy about calling over a flight attendant.

> **Fear of Flying**
>
> Approximately 10% of all people suffer from varying degrees of aerophobia or aviophobia—fear of flying. Fear of flying often includes other phobias, such as fear of heights, fear of enclosed spaces, and fear of being far from home.

There are music and meditation tapes as well as written material specifically designed for calming jangled nerves while in flight. One of the more remarkable treatment options available these days that has a near-perfect cure rate is virtual reality, in which images are transmitted to a headset covering your eyes and ears so you can get used to the sights and sounds of being inside a jetliner, taking off, and landing. You do this with a trained therapist in his or her office. See the Appendix for sources and more information about products and treatment options.

Drunks and crazies. Flying seems to bring out some people's evil twin. Perhaps it is because they drink alcohol out of boredom, or perhaps it is the cramped quarters and reduced levels of service and freebies nowadays. If you have flown lately, you have no doubt witnessed displays of short temper and rude, abusive behavior.

The good thing about beefed-up security these days is that flight attendants are trained to deal with such passengers. If the behavior is extreme, they can subdue the passenger and have the pilot bring the plane down.

If you are caught next to someone who is bothering you or endangering you, do not remain silent. Stand up and leave your seat, if possible.

Press the call button to alert a flight attendant that you are having problems. Tap the shoulders of the passengers in front of you and ask for their help. Make a commotion. Yell, if necessary. Do not sit and be victimized by someone just because you may be physically confined next to him.

Turbulence. Frequent flyers are so accustomed to hearing the pilot announce "turbulence" and instruct us to fasten our seatbelts, that many of us do not take these warnings seriously. Often at the beginning of a flight, the flight attendant will ask you to keep your seatbelt fastened at all times and remain seated. Few people heed this advice unless the ride actually becomes bumpy. But the fact is that many people get injured each year, some fatally, due to airplane turbulence.

You cannot do much to protect yourself from flying objects, but you can certainly fasten your seatbelt securely. Most injuries are caused when people get thrown out of their seats or are in the aisles or bathrooms during a moment of extreme turbulence.

T*he most horrific experience I had with turbulence was once when I flew from Luxembourg to Paris in a storm. The plane went upside down and everyone was praying and reciting their acts of contrition. We all said goodbye and had plenty of time to think about it. Most of the passengers vomited, but I didn't. There was really nothing we could do except wait. The flight attendants were buckled in, and things were flying through the air. There was no help. Fortunately, it was only an hour flight. Everyone who got off the plane that day was very, very ill and traumatized.*

Hijackings. Unfortunately, we Americans now have to think about the possibility that, despite heightened awareness, people with violent intentions may still be able to get on the plane with us. Some of the following good advice comes from Dan McKinnon, former chairman of the Civil Aeronautics Board.

> **Hijacking statistics**
> Your chances of getting hijacked on a plane are 1 in 1,000,000.
> Source: *USA Today*

✈ MARY'S TOP TIPS FOR HIJACKINGS

PREPARE A PLAN OF ACTION WITH YOUR NEIGHBOR. Talk to the passenger nearest you at the beginning of the flight and remind him or her that if everyone acts in concert, a hijacker will not have a chance. Everyone is so hyperconscious about terrorism these days that this is not an unusual topic to bring up.

TAKE ACTION IMMEDIATELY. Like the hijackers' own strategy, the element of surprise is everything. Do not allow the hijackers to organize and get control. Every second you wait lowers your chances of survival. Stand up and charge. Hopefully, others will do the same.

GRAB A MAKESHIFT WEAPON. Books, shoes, rolled-up magazines, briefcases, and bottles are good for attack. Blankets and jackets are good for throwing over their eyes. Shoelaces and belts make good handcuffs.

DO NOT ATTEMPT TO TALK THEM OUT OF IT. They are on a mission, and talking to them only gives them the upper hand and gives them control.

ONCE ON THE GROUND, DO NOT DRAW ATTENTION TO YOURSELF. Hijackers who bring a plane down generally want something—to make a political statement, to cross a border, or to get money—and their only bargaining chips are the passengers. In a hostage situation, you are less likely to be hurt if you shrink back, stay silent, and blend in to the group. Do not ask them for anything. Do not make eye contact with any of the hijackers. Use the bathroom or request a drink only as a very last resort.

DO NOT GET INVOLVED WITH AN OUTSIDE RESCUE ATTEMPT. Remember that your rescuers do not know which among you are the good guys and which are the bad guys. Do not stand up and motion to your rescuers. Lay low.

According to McKinnon, if you survive the first fifteen minutes of a hijacking, you are likely to survive the whole ordeal.

Cruise Travel

I love travel aboard cruise ships, and I do it all the time. In many respects, cruise travel is the safest of all modes. If there is political trouble brewing in a country, cruise ships simply redesign their routes to avoid conflicts. Many people do not realize that cruise ships are, in essence, floating nations. The captain is president of that country outside of the three-mile maritime boundary. If any ship had to go to war, it is equipped with enough ammunition to defend itself.

Cruise ships have medical facilities, jails, security personnel, educational and fitness resources, food and sanitation, childcare, and built-in entertainment and enrichment programs. There are uniformed and undercover security people onboard every ship, and the office is open round the clock, every day.

Every passenger on a cruise ship participates in a safety drill and lecture. In the unlikely event of evacuation, cruise ships have enough well-trained staff and survival equipment to get you through the crisis alive.

Cruise ships adhere to the same security policies as airplanes. All passengers are screened and their bags checked. Use the same common sense and guidelines for cruise travel as you do when preparing to travel by air. Oftentimes, security will collect any knives or sharp instruments over 5 inches long. They confiscate them, place them in the hold during the voyage, and then give them back the last night, prior to disembarkation, so passengers can pack them in their luggage. Therefore, it is perhaps wise to be extra vigilant on the *last night* of a cruise.

> **An Avoidable Travel Illness**
>
> Sexually transmitted diseases are among the top five most common travel illnesses.

Statistically, there is very little crime aboard cruise ships. You are more likely to encounter problems in ports, which I will cover next chapter.

✈ MARY'S TOP TIPS FOR CRUISE TRAVEL

PAY ATTENTION TO SAFETY DRILLS. Learn the best routes from your cabin to the lifeboats and fire exits.

HAVE ENOUGH LIFE JACKETS IN YOUR CABIN. If there are not enough life jackets in your cabin for everyone, ask your cabin steward to provide them.

USE DEADBOLTS AND OTHER LOCKS PROVIDED BY THE CRUISE LINE. And make certain that the door to the adjoining cabin is locked.

DO NOT USE THE CABIN SAFE. The best way to protect your valuables is to lock them in the ship's safety deposit box. Never use the safe provided in your cabin. Keep other valuables locked inside your luggage with a combination lock.

PREVENT FIRES. Fires are the greatest hazard of cruise travel. Do not smoke in bed. Make sure curling irons and other plug-ins are turned off and unplugged before you leave your cabin. And never throw a burning cigarette overboard, as it can fly back into an open window or open veranda and start a fire.

USE HANDRAILS. Decks can become unexpectedly slippery.

USE SUNSCREEN AND WEAR A HAT. Avoid the misery of overdoing it in the sun in the first few days of your trip.

USE ALCOHOL WISELY. Sea motion can have a synergistic effect on alcohol, so wait until you have your sea legs before consuming alcohol.

BRING YOUR VALUES AND JUDGMENT ABOARD. Passengers tend to engage in riskier behaviors at sea where young, attractive crewmembers abound. If you are looking for *amore,* remember that you are not the first passenger this handsome or beautiful crewmember has encountered. Use protection, and do not invite anyone to your cabin whom you would not invite into your home. Also, protect yourself from a broken heart. Chances are good that you will never see this person again after the cruise is over.

DO NOT GIVE YOUR CABIN NUMBER TO STRANGERS. Never leave cabin keys unattended. Check keys with the ship's steward if you plan to be at the pool.

AVOID THE BAGGAGE HOLDING AREA. There is really no reason to go down there. It is the only dark, unpopulated place on a cruise ship.

HAVE MEDICINES AND ESSENTIALS WITH YOU ON THE LAST NIGHT. Be prepared for the fact that the crew will take your luggage from you and place it in the holding area the night before you disembark, so keep with you any items essential to your health and safety.

C lients of mine were sailing aboard one of the "love boats" and became well acquainted with another couple. During the voyage, they shared lots of information about their houses, lifestyles, family, etc. When my clients returned home, they discovered they had been ripped off. Their new 32-inch state-of-the-art TV, stereo, and DVD player was gone! They traced it back to dishing out way too much information to their newfound "friends" on the luxury liner.

The Arrival Payoff

More unpleasant situations have happened to me in transit than at the destinations to which I was traveling, and I would guess that this is true for most frequent travelers. Although getting there is part of the fun, the payoff is to finally arrive. Now the real fun can begin.

Pinched Disks

Cameras are one of the most commonly stolen items. The loss of a digital camera, however, could mean the loss of hundreds of images stored on your disk. If you cannot afford to lose your cherished photos, remove your disk and keep it separate from your camera.

4

Arriving at Your Destination
Making the Best of Your Vacation

They say that getting there is half the fun. But for me, arriving at my destination is the absolute best. It never fails to arouse in me a sense of heightened excitement, newness, and adventure. I love landing in a strange and exotic place, settling into my new surroundings, and then getting out into the world ready for discovery and fresh experiences.

In unfamiliar environments, people tend to let down their guard. Being on vacation does not mean taking a vacation from common sense! If you keep health and safety in your conscious mind once you arrive, it will make for a much better vacation, free of unpleasant incidents.

Just as your destination dictates the type of clothing you need to pack, it also spells out the kind of precautions you can take to make your vacation worry free.

Camping and Motorhoming

Because of our weak economy and people's security concerns, many Americans are choosing domestic travel over foreign travel, and land travel over air travel. Camping and motorhoming are great ways to vacation if you have children with you or want maximum flexibility about where to go and how long to stay there.

As I have mentioned, driving is the most dangerous mode of travel. On the other hand, camping is generally quite safe. Here are some things to keep in mind on a camping vacation.

✈ Mary's Top Tips for Camping

KEEP VALUABLES HIDDEN AND LOCKED IN YOUR VEHICLE. There is scant security in campgrounds, so do not leave cameras, video recorders, documents, or money at your campsite while you are away enjoying the great outdoors.

TALK TO FELLOW CAMPERS. Campgrounds are unusually open and friendly communities. Fellow campers are gold mines of information about local sights, restaurants, and cultural attractions. Talk to your neighbors to get good ideas about best ways to spend your time. They can also alert you to campground hazards such as recent thievery or wild animal incidents.

EDUCATE YOURSELF ABOUT LOCAL FLORA AND FAUNA. Whether it is scorpions or deer ticks, rattlers or black bears, jellyfish or alligators, spend some time finding out which plants, insects, and animals are dangerous and how to avoid them.

DO NOT VENTURE OUT ALONE. Remember the buddy system when you were a kid? It still applies. However, if you love solo running, hiking, biking, or kayaking, then make certain you tell a companion where you are going and when you plan to be back. Bring a cell phone just in case. You can also get walkie-talkies now that have a four-mile range.

FOLLOW CAMPGROUND GUIDELINES. It sounds like a no-brainer, but people get careless with food and fire when they are camping. Protect yourself, your companions, and others, because animal attacks and forest fires are on the rise.

DO NOT LEAVE PETS ALONE AT YOUR CAMPSITE. A tied-up animal is food for large predators and can become a nuisance to neighboring campers as well.

When people are vacationing close to nature, the greatest dangers are nature-related: getting lost on a hike, running out of food or water, strolling among the poison ivy, burning in the sun, losing your balance on a rocky ledge. My advice here is the same as everywhere else: Use common sense. Always have a small supply of water and food in a daypack in case your one-hour hike turns into an all-day adventure. Bring protective clothing, especially in the mountains, where weather can shift dramatically in a matter of minutes. Never drink water out of a stream, no matter how sparkling it looks. Respect the power of nature. Here are other items it would be wise to have along:

Campground Etiquette

- Keep noise to a minimum.
- Don't let pets or children become nuisances.
- Leave environment cleaner than when you arrived.
- Use your campsite as is. Do not clear new areas.
- If you arrive at night, keep your headlights low.
- If an empty campsite has already been staked out with a chair or other object, its occupants are probably touring for the day. Find a different site.
- Obey the 5 mph speed limit. Use low gear if your vehicle has trouble going that slowly.
- Do not throw lit or unlit cigarettes on the ground.

Rugged Camping Necessities Checklist

- ☑ Updated first aid and emergency medical kit
- ☑ Safety flares for remote roadside emergencies
- ☑ Walkie-talkies with several-mile range
- ☑ Extra bulbs and batteries for flashlight and walkie-talkies
- ☑ Bug and sun protectors
- ☑ Three-day supply of dried food
- ☑ Water purification tablets and collapsible plastic jug with lid

- ☑ Multi-tool
- ☑ Compass and topographical map
- ☑ Matches
- ☑ Rain poncho that could double as emergency one-man tent
- ☑ Plastic bags, plastic sheeting, duct tape
- ☑ Roll of toilet paper

Arriving in a Foreign Land

If you have not had a lot of experience traveling outside this country, you might be surprised by the long lines, paperwork, and unfamiliar procedures that greet you as soon as you arrive by ship, train, bus, or plane in a foreign land.

New Passport Regulations

Since 9/11, some countries have modified their passport requirements. For example, Venezuela and Indonesia will not even let you into the country now if your passport is due to expire within six months. The Netherlands, on the other hand, will bar you from entry if your passport is not *at least* six months old. Know the updated rules by contacting the country's embassy in Washington, DC.

Immigration

First stop is immigration. You will need to present the proper documentation: always a passport, and often an entrance visa as well. Certain countries, such as Egypt, Turkey, and Australia, require a visa. Entry visas are pre-stamped on your passport. You have to send away for a visa ninety days prior to travel. Having the required documentation *before* you travel is another great reason to book your trip through a travel agent, who will make certain that you arrive at your destination prepared. See the Appendix for addresses and websites of offices that issue passports and visas, as well as "expeditors," who can cut down your waiting time significantly—for an added fee, of course.

In the event that you find yourself without a tourist card, in the case of Mexico, or a visa or a valid passport, you will be sent back to the last country you were in, in order to secure the needed paperwork. That could take days or weeks, and could cost you a small fortune.

O *ne of my travel misadventures happened a few years ago in Greece. As I was going through immigration, I was singled out by an official who placed a large X in yellow chalk on my new black leather shoulder bag. He shoved me into a private room and left me there alone for hours. No one came into the room to tell me why I was being held there. Being separated from my travel companions and knowing the transfer buses were leaving to go into Athens without me, I began to panic. Since no one had come to interrogate me—or to rescue me— I found a side door, slipped outside, and escaped into a back alley, running to find my way to the bus terminal. I literally jumped on the first bus I saw—I didn't care where it was going. Fortunately, it was a bus that went into Athens. To this day, I never knew what they wanted from me or why they singled me out. I also don't know what they might have done to me if I had been caught escaping.*

Claiming Your Baggage

Baggage carousels and baggage handling procedures are pretty much the same at all major airports, whether American or overseas. Follow the same precautions in a foreign airport as you would anywhere else. Always mark your luggage with a distinctive tie or strap. Only about one out of every ten airports I have traveled to has an attendant who compares your bag tag with your ID tag to verify that you are picking up the same luggage you checked.

So That's Where It Went...

Scottsboro, Alabama, is home to the Unclaimed Baggage Center. Opened in 1970, it sells everything from diamond-studded cuff links to boxers and half-used bottles of perfume. The Center has an agreement with most U.S. airlines to resell unclaimed luggage and its contents for half the original value. Clothing is washed, pressed, or dry-cleaned. The store's treasures come from unclaimed passenger bags and airfreight, and items left at airports or on airplanes. More than a million caps, shirts, and cameras are sold each year. Designer clothes, electronics, and luggage are other popular sellers.

Money Down the Drain

Foreign countries will not let you take more than $400 in purchased goods out of their country without paying hefty taxes on these items, and other items cannot be taken at all. Always keep this in mind when you shop overseas. I once purchased fresh, exotic bags of spices in a Middle Eastern market, but I had to abandon them all at the border. Apparently, spices are considered food.

S *ooner or later, your baggage will get lost if you travel frequently enough. On a cruise ship tour I was leading, one unfortunate but good-natured man in our group lost his luggage. The airlines could find no trace of it. He had his essential overnight things with him, but no clothes except for what he was wearing. We decided to help him make the best of the situation. At every country we visited, he purchased a new outfit— the native costume. He was the life of the party modeling his international wardrobe for us every day. At the end of the cruise, they found his bag. It had been sitting in an unbooked cabin next to his the entire time.*

Customs

Going through customs is usually noneventful, but occasionally there will be something about you—your luggage, your expression, maybe your attitude, who knows?—that compels a customs agent to pull you aside and give you and your bags a thorough check. Here are some ways to avoid that scenario, or to make the best of it.

✈ MARY'S TOP TIPS FOR GOING THROUGH CUSTOMS

IF YOU DRESS LIKE A SLOB, EXPECT TO BE TREATED LIKE A SLOB. Customs agents judge passengers by how they look. If you are dirty, smelly, and unkempt, expect to be stopped and searched.

YOUR LUGGAGE TELLS A LOT ABOUT YOU. If you are going to bring designer bags wrapped in protective plastic, you will be stopped at customs. The same is true if you have a hippie backpack or old duffels held together by duct tape.

BE AWARE OF DUTY-FREE PURCHASES. Travelers who take advantage of cheap prices at the duty-free shop at the departing airport often forget that there is a dollar limit on items they can bring into another country. Avoid hefty fees by knowing these limits *before* you spend your hard-earned money.

SMILE, SMILE, SMILE. Have a pleasant demeanor, and you can lessen your chances of being singled out by customs agents.

DO NOT GET SEPARATED FROM YOUR BAGS. When I am pulled aside at customs, I never allow the agents to take my briefcase away from me where I cannot keep my eye on it. It is my livelihood, I explain to them, and has all of my work in it. If they argue, I remain firm. In this situation, request that a clerk accompany you back to the room or behind the screen where agents have your bag. Do not lose visual contact with your possessions.

I *have seen many an unhappy tourist who started or ended a vacation by getting stung with "gotchas." Gotchas are unexpected airport transportation fees, taxes you've never heard of, exit fees—you name it. These require cold, hard cash—no checks, no credit cards. Travel agents should alert you to these beforehand. If you do not have cash on hand—American dollars are always welcome, by the way— you will have to schlep you luggage all the way through the airport to the nearest ATM and back before the authorities will let you through security. Don't let this happen to you. Arrive prepared.*

Getting to Your Hotel

The hardest part of every trip outside the United States is getting from the airport to the hotel. If you are lucky, your hotel will have its own van that shuttles guests to and from the airport. If not, the absolute safest, fastest, and most reliable way to get to your hotel, if you can afford the extra bucks, is to hire a private transportation company. These are the people you see holding up little signs with last names written on them when you walk out of customs. You or your travel agent must arrange ahead of time for private, direct transportation to your hotel.

Another way to get to your hotel is by taxi. It is not as easy as it might seem.

Creative Cabbies

In many countries, taxi fare is negotiable and variable. Never settle into a cab until you have negotiated a price with the driver. Ask him how much it will cost, and get him to agree to a specific fare before you become his passenger. Otherwise, you may be taken for more of a ride than you bargained for.

✈ MARY'S TOP TIPS FOR TAXI TRAVEL FROM THE AIRPORT

BE AN INFORMED TOURIST. Email or phone the hotel where you will be staying ahead of time, and find out the distance in kilometers from the airport to your hotel. Ask how much you can expect to pay for a taxi.

OBEY THE TAXI "SYSTEM." At foreign airports, and many domestic ones as well, you may need to stand in line while a taxi conductor or expeditor takes down your destination and arranges for a taxi to take you there. These systems are set up for maximum efficiency. Obey them. If you try to hail a cab on your own, you are asking for trouble.

HAVE THE TAXI CONDUCTOR TALK TO THE CABBIE. Show the conductor a brochure or the address of your hotel. Ask him how much money it will cost, and make certain that he, not you, tells the taxi driver where you will be going. Also, ask him what is expected in the way of tipping.

JOT DOWN THE DRIVER'S NAME AND ID NUMBER. Taxi drivers the world over have meters, photographs, and ID numbers clearly visible. If you are in a developed country and your taxi driver does not have these items in plain sight, do not get in the cab.

A mericans are often surprised when they are in a foreign taxi and the driver pulls over to pick up another fare. This is common practice all over the world, except in our country. The first time this happened to me I didn't know what to make of it. Now, I just relax and allow extra time to get to my appointments when I cab it in Europe.

There's No Place Like Prison?

If you are bored of staying in hotels, Sweden offers rooms in prison at a good nightly rate. Or maybe you would rather sleep in a Swedish house completely made out of ice. In Italy, you can stay in a convent. In Costa Rica, try sleeping in a treehouse. Ireland has its castles, and Spain lets you catch some zzz's in a cave—with free laundry service included. If you have ever wanted to sleep inside a water tower, go to Germany. These are just a few of the wacky accommodations you can find when you type "unusual accommodations" into Google.

Hotels, Inns, and Resorts

I have had my share of unpleasant and scary experiences in every kind of accommodation during my years as a travel writer and expert. Whether you stay in a five-star resort in Hawaii or a four-room inn in Morocco, there are certain precautions you can take to make your stay safer and more enjoyable.

Some of my earlier advice bears repeating at this point. Did you remember to Pack Your ACT? *A* stands for Attitude, *C* for Common sense, and *T* for Tact. When you arrive at your destination, it is time to unpack your attitude. Do not expect your accommodations to be your home away from home. Do not expect the same creature comforts you are used to. Adopting that frame of mind will go a long way toward making your stay more enjoyable.

Getting a Room

The hotel industry is a service industry. The people who work in hotels want you to be safe and they want your return business. I take advantage of that relationship at the offset to negotiate better rooms and better prices.

✈ MARY'S TOP TIPS FOR GETTING A ROOM

MAKE AN ALLIANCE WITH THE DESK CLERK. When I get to the front desk, I lean forward and say quietly, "I'm a tired, single traveler. What's the best room you can offer me at this rate?" They always take a second look at their computer and, more times than not, will find me a bigger, quieter room with a nice view.

FREQUENT TRAVELER CARDS WORK. Because I travel a lot, I have Preferred Customer cards for many of the big-name hotels. When I present my number up front, hotel clerks jump through hoops to find me better deals and rooms, because they consider me a loyal customer.

ASK FOR A ROOM IN A SAFE LOCATION. Request a room that is not on the first floor. In small foreign hotels, scope out back alleyways, fire escapes, balconies, and rooftops that could provide access for an intruder.

I was in Venice a couple of years ago staying in a small hotel. I was up on the third floor, sitting outside after a long day of sightseeing, writing in my journal, with my Walkman and headset on. Along comes a bellhop, finished with his shift, who says, "Would you like me to show you Venice?" No, I said, I've just seen Venice and I'm writing in my journal. He insisted that, No, I didn't understand. I was coming with him to see Venice. At this point, I refused again and said I was tired and was going to bed. Naïvely, I opened my hotel room door to go in and he pushed me inside and forced himself in as well. I kicked him hard and, somehow, got such a charge of adrenaline that I was able to push him back through the door and double lock it from within. However, the story didn't end there. My room faced out onto a small canal, and all night long that man stood across the alleyway below and threw rocks across the canal at my wooden balcony door, yelling threats alternating with mournful professions of love. Naturally, it was a hot humid night and I was steaming inside, in more ways than one. The next morning I called management and asked them to escort me downstairs and out of that hotel forever.

Room Safety

The above story illustrates why you should never enter your hotel room when someone is lurking outside in the hallway. Sadly, though, most hotel crime is committed by people who have your key: hotel employees. There are wonderful mail-order and online vendors that sell every security item and gadget under the sun. If you are traveling to a particularly danger-ous country, check out these companies for such items as door locks, video monitors, and other ingenious devices designed for hotel-room safety. I have included some of the best ones in the Appendix.

✈ Mary's Top Tips for Hotel Room Safety

Politely ask the desk clerk not to blurt out your room number. At the check-in desk, I have found that they are exceptionally thoughtful in this regard.

Ask the desk clerk to swipe your room key twice. Occasionally, a key from the previous guest might still be activated.

Remove the top coverlet from your bed. Hotel sheets are washed daily, but bedspreads are almost never laundered. Like airplane seats and head cushions, if those bedspreads could talk, you would not want them in your room.

Always latch or chain-lock your door from the inside. Get into the habit of doing this, even when you are stopping in briefly to pick something up.

Invest in a rubber doorstop. Lightweight and small, a doorstop will halt an intruder in his tracks.

Keep the Do Not Disturb sign on your door. After your room has been cleaned, hang the sign on your door when you go out to make potential intruders think your room is occupied.

Take your money belt into the bathroom with you. I have gotten into the habit of doing this. While I am singing in the shower, I do not want someone slipping quickly into and out of my room to snatch my money, documents, and credit cards.

Do not order pizza or other take-out from an outside establishment. The last thing you want is for strangers outside the hotel to know where you are staying.

Keep your hotel room key or card next to the door. If you would have to exit quickly in the event of a fire or other emergency, you want that key readily accessible.

I was sleeping in my hotel at the Los Angeles airport when I was suddenly awakened by what I thought was an attacker pouncing on my bed. After I was thrown against the wall with my king bed mattress following me, I realized I was in the middle of a very violent earthquake. After what seemed like forever, as the TV, remote control, and various other loose objects settled down, I ran to the front door of my suite, opened it, and stepped out to peer across the atrium. Voila! The door shut and I locked myself out of my room! Here I am in my pajamas, no eyeglasses, no purse, no room key, and it's 4:25 in the morning. Since then, I always remember to keep my room key near the door so I can grab it for quick exits.

Hotel Safes

Never, ever use the safe in your hotel room to stash your valuable belongings. Why do I say this? Because hotel service people—from hotel security and chambermaids to laundry people, guest services, and bell hops—all have access to your room. All over the world, chambermaids are traditionally underpaid, uneducated foreigners. Once in your room, they can easily figure out the four-digit code for your room safe. Your code is usually a familiar number—the last four digits of your social security number, or your birthday, for example. Your personal information is extremely easy to obtain, and with it, your jewelry, camera, and documents.

There are two better options. If you brought along valuable jewelry, which I strongly advise against, keep it in the hotel vault behind the front desk. This is the absolute safest place to keep your precious possessions. The other option is to store documents, credit card duplicates, and other items you do not want to lose in your own suitcase, bound with a strap, and locked with a combination lock. I have never had anything stolen from any hotel room since I began doing this.

O ne time, I was traveling with a Greek girlfriend of mine, heading to Athens, when a very suave, drop-dead-handsome Greek man invited us to stay at the five-star hotel where he was staying. Being young, adventurous, and naïve, we had been planning on just winging it, and had nothing booked. We agreed to go with this debonair stranger, who was really hitting it off with my friend. When the three of us arrived, I asked the front desk to put my money and credit cards in their hotel vault. The person told me it was full. A five-star hotel's vault? Full? I should have been suspicious right then and there, but instead I excused myself and went up to our room, put my valuables under my pillow, and slept straight through until late the next morning. Meanwhile, my friend had gone off with her handsome Greek. It wasn't until I was getting on the ferry the next day that I discovered all of my cash was gone. Not my cards, just my cash. To this day, I am certain that the handsome man and the hotel were in cahoots, because several days later when I returned to pick up my girlfriend, I saw Mr. Handsome walking out of the hotel vault, like he owned the joint. How his people got my money out from under my pillow while I slept, I will never know. But I have always suspected that I was gassed and then robbed. When I reported the theft to the authorities, they said, "Yeah, we're familiar with this."

Hotel Restaurants and Bars

No matter where in the world I am traveling, I always try to book a hotel that has a small restaurant or coffee shop on premises. If I will be staying in a small hotel in a foreign country, I find one that has a restaurant next door or on the same street. You do not want to be wandering unfamiliar streets in the early morning or late at night when hunger beckons.

Hotel bars can be good places to unwind after a long day of traveling, sightseeing, or working. Having a drink in your hotel lets you take the elevator up to your room—no driving, which is a plus.

The downside of hotel bars is that they are sometimes havens for low-life characters, as my story below illustrates.

I was in a very respectable hotel in Fort Lauderdale on a business trip recently. A girlfriend of mine was sharing my room and went down to the bar to unwind with a glass of wine. I was tired, so I stayed in our room. It got later and later. When she didn't show up, I went to sleep. At four in the morning, she came stumbling in with a big bash on her head. What had happened is this: A man had sat down next to her at the bar. When she had left her glass on the bar to visit the ladies' room, he had slipped that date rape drug into her drink. We called security and the police and had to take her to the emergency room. She had bruises underneath her dress and was in bad shape emotionally. On returning to the hotel later that same day, we discovered the man had checked out. Moral of the story: Ladies, never leave your drink unattended. Such criminals sometimes work in pairs. While one is asking you to dance, another might be drugging your cocktail.

Being a Tourist in a Foreign Country

No matter how hard you try to blend in, anywhere you go in the world, natives will look at you and think *American*. I do not know what it is, but Americans cannot help looking like Americans. This has its pros and cons, depending on the country. When you are sightseeing, shopping, and traveling around in a foreign country, keep your antennas up, because you will stand out in the crowd, and that could mean that you will be targeted for theft, inflated charges, or worse.

Ports of Call

I have had a great deal of experience with cruise travel, because organizing cruise tours is one of my specialties. Except in the States, ports of call are geared to the cruise tourist. Shops, galleries, and nice eateries are usually within walking distance. Sometimes gorgeous beaches and reefs are too. Because they cater to the day-tourist crowd, ports of call are generally safe places to walk around.

Cruise ships sail by night and dock by day. Before you disembark, talk to the tour operator onboard to get a good idea of what you can expect to find and do in the port city. They know it all: good (and bad) places to eat, neighborhoods to avoid, local customs, tipping procedures, and more. Spend some time jotting down notes and being prepared before you disembark.

Immigration and customs are the same at ports as they are at airports. Follow my commonsense tips, above, and you will sail through the bureaucratic and security checkpoints seamlessly.

Rip-Ups and Rip-Offs

Never rip up your credit card carbons and then toss them into the trash. Save them and keep them with your important documents. Not only will you have a nice record of your trip's expenses, but this prevents a wily thief from fishing the pieces out of the trash can and reusing your info.

Water Stop

Drinking lots of water when traveling is so essential to health that I always keep a ready supply of bottled water in my cruise ship cabin. Buying those little bottles onboard can get expensive, however. I ask the cruise staff where they buy inexpensive bottled water. I often follow them into town to stock up in little neighborhood grocery stores and save a bundle of money.

I was cruising on a ship as a guest of the Greek government when the cruise ship sailing next to us, the Achille Lauro, was hijacked by two terrorists. The captain called me into his office and told me what had happened. We switched courses and wandered at sea for three days until our provisions ran out and we had no choice but to pull into the port of Cairo. Whom did we dock right next to? The Achille Lauro, with the terrorists still aboard! The Egyptian army were everywhere. We were accompanied off our ship with officials every six feet, taking us under their arms and walking with us down the gangway. It was terrifying.

✈ MARY'S TOP TIPS FOR PORTS OF CALL

BE A SAVVY TOURIST. Get all the information you can about the port city before your cruise, and also ask the ship's tour director.

CONSIDER DAY-TRIP OPTIONS. Cruise ships always offer a variety of day-trips, such as snorkeling expeditions, tours of historic sites, and nature hikes. Ports of call offer these too. But they can be expensive and even tiring. It may be more economical and fun to buy a map and hire a local taxi driver for a half day to take you around to all the sites that are not within walking distance.

LEAVE VALUABLES ON THE SHIP. There is no reason to walk around in a foreign country with expensive equipment, jewelry, and bundles of cash. The ship is the safest place for valuables.

STAY ALERT. Be aware that petty thieves could be waiting for your ship's arrival. When you are in a crowd, thieves' modus operandi is usually to cause a commotion while a partner picks your pocket.

I *was in a Tunisian* souk, *or marketplace, when I saw one of the women from our cruise in the shop next to me. Out of the corner of my eye, I noticed some kind of commotion, and then it dawned on me that I saw this woman's feet and some men were carrying her away. They had literally thrown a black veil over her and were stealing her away. I called to a couple of guys in our group and we went running after her. When we caught up to them, the men set her down and said they were just showing her some fabric! We may have saved this poor woman from a life of white slavery. She and the rest of us had been warned very specifically to stay out of the shops where the locals sell carpets, but this woman did not heed the cruise director's advice. I think we all learned a valuable lesson that day to pay attention when they say: "Do not wander off from your group while shopping in the* souk." *They mean it.*

Remote Resorts

There are wonderful resorts now, for families and singles, children, gay people, nudists, elderly—you name it—that are designed to be self-contained. These Club Med–style resorts are usually sited in gorgeous, remote parts of countries, well separated from the local culture—sometimes by a cyclone fence!

Self-contained resorts have everything a vacationer would want: restaurants, bars, shops, entertainment, five activities a day, fun classes and educational workshops, and more. If you find yourself in one of these places, chances

When You Gotta Go, You Gotta Pay

Public toilets in Europe and elsewhere are not free. To unlock the stall door requires a few coins. If there is an attendant, he or she will expect you to pay for paper towels. In remote parts of Israel and Arab countries, little Bedouin children sometimes block entry until you give them a shekel. Always keep a few coins on hand, because when you gotta go, you gotta go. Also, carry your own folded serviettes in a fanny pack.

International Tipping Quiz

Rarely is tipping considered an insult. The appreciation of money is universal. However, every culture has its own tipping norms, and it is possible to offend a waiter by tipping too little or too much. See if you can match the country with its tipping expectations.

Australia & New Zealand
Japan
Germany & France
China

a. Do not tip.
b. Tipping is rare.
c. 10–15% usually added to bill.
d. No tipping, but foreigners are routinely charged more.

Answers: b, a, c, d

are you chose it because you did not want to experience a lot of native culture.

That is okay. One advantage to self-contained resorts is that they are quite safe. Except for the petty thievery, it is unlikely that you will find yourself a victim of a crime.

Having said that, I should point out that if you are getting stir crazy and want to explore other parts of the island or country, get all the information you can before venturing out. The resort is staffed with professionals whose aim it is to serve you. The local community might not be as geared toward tourists and their needs.

Changing Money

I have said it before, and will say it again: Never carry more than $50 in any kind of currency at any time. You really do not need a lot of cash. Use Visa or MasterCard for most purchases. Use American Express for large purchases (because Amex automatically insures your purchases for theft). Use travelers checks mainly to exchange currency. Taxicab drivers and many shops and restaurants will not accept travelers checks these days. Shops that do accept them usually charge a vendor's fee.

Another great option these days is the new prepaid "money card," which offers the safest travel cash. Money cards are a new option offered through Visa and to AAA members. You load the card with a certain amount of cash before leaving home and choose a PIN. You can draw local currency cash from over 800,000 ATMs that accept Visa worldwide. Benefits: A thief cannot forge a name on a money card. It has no value without your password. Also, it will not lead you into temptation if you do not overload it upfront.

L ike an investment portfolio, it is good to have a lot of variety in your money belt. In Europe, my friend was out of cash altogether and went to an ATM. Guess what? It didn't work. Out of order. In that situation, credit cards and debit cards were useless, and we were flat out of cash. Luckily, I had a travelers check on me, which saved the day.

Before you left home, you should have gotten about $50 in foreign currency. If you did not, you will always find currency exchanges right in the airport. Airport currency exchanges are good places to get some pocket money for cabs or whatnot, and usually have the best exchange rates. The disadvantage is that you could waste a lot of time waiting in long lines, because everyone else who just got off the plane had the same idea.

Change bureaus are everywhere in major foreign cities, and even in small towns. This is where you change travelers checks into the local currency. They are often open twenty-four hours a day. Use common sense if visiting one at night, where opportunistic thieves could be lurking nearby.

ATMs are also universal, but I have found that credit cards do not work well at all of them. Get a debit card or the above-mentioned prepaid money card instead, memorize your PIN number, and make sure that you put enough cash in your account before you leave home. Before you stick your card into an ATM, verify that it will accept a debit card from your bank.

Don't Shoot

Believe it or not, photographing is often considered taboo, depending on where you are. For example, in Arab countries, women should never be photographed, and photographing people in general is frowned upon. In many Persian Gulf countries, ports, airports, and government buildings are sensitive subject matter. The picturesque old buildings you love may be regarded with embarrassment by many locals as relics from a backward past. Know the local customs before indulging in Kodak moments.

I have joined the e-generation of online bankers and I love it for traveling. On even the remotest of islands, I can visit an Internet café, log on to my Wells Fargo bank account, and see within seconds exactly where my money has been deducted. Then I take a printout. It is so cool. Your statement is in U.S. currency. One time in Greece someone got hold of a credit card carbon and I had a $426 charge on my account that I could not have made—because I was flying back home at the time of purchase! Thanks to e-banking, I knew the precise time and place of the scam and reported it immediately.

Sightseeing

There are many ways to see amazing sights at your new destination. Above all, do it safely by arming yourself with the best information you can obtain from the internet, books, your travel agent, and from your hotel concierge.

Organized group tours are extremely safe, and have the added benefit of a knowledgeable English-speaking guide. If you decide to hoof it on your own, buy a self-guided book so you do not miss out on the good information you would have gotten in the lecture. I love to use local tour guides. They are talented and often have insider information that I could not have gotten elsewhere.

I have found that a great way to get around is by taxi or by local transportation companies, and you can sometimes hire them by the half day.

If you are feeling adventurous and want to save money, go ahead and use public transportation: buses, trains, subways, and ferries. Hotel concierges can give you tips on public transportation dos and don'ts. Take advantage of their expertise, and above all, heed their advice. The same metro that is perfectly pleasant by day could turn into a tunnel of terror by night.

W hen I was in high school, I had the opportunity to live in Iran for two months. Had I done my homework better, I would have had a much better experience. I was a blue-eyed blonde who wore skirts above my knees and didn't have a clue about the local culture. One time, riding on a public bus with my roommate, I got separated from her when she got off, while I was shoved to the back of the bus by a small pack of men. I screamed and made a commotion, but they were louder with wild coyote-type sounds, crowding around me, trying to undress me, mauling me. My girlfriend managed to get the attention of the driver and rescue me, but barely.

✈ MARY'S TOP TIPS FOR SIGHTSEEING

TAKE A MAP. Do not assume that you can find your way back to your hotel after a long day of sightseeing.

BRING A POSTCARD OF THE HOTEL WHERE YOU ARE STAYING. If your hotel does not have one, then jot down the name, address, and phone number of the hotel and keep it in your money belt.

BRING WATER, A SNACK, A PHRASE BOOK, AND AN INTERNATIONAL CELL PHONE. You never know when you could get lost, be out longer than planned, or get into trouble. Be prepared for any circumstance.

DRESS APPROPRIATELY. Wear comfortable shoes and dress conservatively.

KNOW AND RESPECT LOCAL CUSTOMS. Never feel self-conscious about asking your concierge such questions as: Is it appropriate to enter a mosque or cathedral at any time? Are there rules you can tell me about photographing, tipping, or haggling?

Shopping

One of the great pleasures of travel is shopping in an exotic place far from home. Here are some commonsense guidelines.

✈ Mary's Top Tips for Shopping

UNDERSTAND THE CURRENCY. The way most Americans get ripped off is by being charged the wrong amount or not counting their change after a purchase. The fact that this new currency looks like Monopoly money is no reason to simply hand the vendor a wad and trust him to do the right thing.

DO NOT CARRY A PURSE. Keep your money and credit cards next to your body, and keep your hands free, if possible.

DO NOT BUY MORE THAN YOU CAN CARRY. I am talking about large, heavy bags that you have to lug around with you the whole day. Consider, too, that you will have to bring this stuff home with you on your return trip. Hopefully, you remembered to pack a collapsible suitcase to accommodate your new treasures.

INFORM YOURSELF ABOUT HAGGLING. In some cultures, haggling is expected. In other cultures, and even in some areas of certain cities, it is considered rude. Ask your concierge whether and how to do it.

Eating Out

I love to eat local cuisine in local restaurants. I often ask the concierge and other hotel employees where *they* like to eat, and why. To avoid getting sick, do not drink the local tap water and do not drink beverages with ice. Never eat street food, because that is a recipe for gastronomic disaster.

The two most challenging aspects of eating out in a foreign county are ordering and tipping. If you attempt to speak a few phrases in the native tongue, chances are your waiter will appreciate the effort and speak to you in English. Do not expect the level of service you are used to in the States. In some countries, such as Russia, for example, waiter service is sometimes very minimal. If you are mentally prepared for this, you will not lose your cool. As for tipping, it is fine to ask the waiter if service is included. Better yet, find out the local tipping expectations before you even leave your hotel.

> ### Southpaw Taboos
>
> If you are in a Muslim country or restaurant, never pick up food with your left hand. It is extremely taboo and people around you will view you with disgust and even hostility. If you are left-handed, eat with your right hand. Good luck!

Getting Ill or Injured

Most Americans are amazed to discover that you can buy just about any medication over the counter in other countries, medications that require a prescription at home. As I advised earlier, a first-aid kit, a supply of broad-spectrum antibiotics, and anti-diarrhea medicine are great allies that will serve you in most situations.

However, if something happens to you during your trip that requires you to see a doctor, never fear. You have come armed with your medical insurance number, emergency medical telephone numbers, and your common sense.

> ### Travel Sickness
>
> Half to three quarters of the estimated 40 million Yanks who travel abroad each year experience some kind of minor medical problem. The chance of being stricken increases for the 8 million Americans who travel each year to a developing country.

Doctors the world over are in their profession to help patients, and you will probably find that they are the same as doctors in the United States—only cheaper! By the way, it is customary in most foreign clinics to pay cash for a visit to the doctor.

How to Avoid Being an Ugly American

The reason people become ugly Americans is because they did not do their homework and they forgot to pack their ACT: Attitude, Common Sense, and Tact. Uninformed Americans, unprepared for the differences in customs and cultures, tend to get frustrated, impatient, and downright rude at times. Take a little time to learn about the country you are visiting. Remind yourself that this is not your home. And remember that there are going to be many different kinds of experiences—which is why you traveled to a foreign country to begin with.

How to Avoid Being a Crime Victim

When you are a tourist in a foreign country, you will stand out. Once again, staying alert and using good old-fashioned common sense are your best allies. Do not wear ostentatious jewelry. Do not carry a purse. Never get into an unmarked taxicab. Be alert for scam artists who cause a commotion to divert your attention while a partner lifts your bags, picks your pockets, or makes off with your camera. Know where you are going. If your concierge or travel agent warns you about a dangerous area, do not go there. Always carry a cell phone. If you get caught in a dangerous situation, cause a commotion. Yell the word *Police!* That is an international call for help, in every language.

> ### Ghost Movies, Ghost Calls
>
> Never leave a hotel without first examining your bill. I have been zinged several times by bills that claimed I watched movies or made long-distance calls. I use my cell phone for all phone calls—great for dinner reservations—and I never check out of my hotel without visiting the front desk.

I n markets all over Europe and the Middle East, beware of bands of gypsy children, Bedouin children, and charming little imps with musical instruments, waving colorful veils, who crowd around you and want to take your picture or sell you trinkets. These little professionals-in-training are raised to spot tourist-victims. While you are transfixed by their bubbly energy and curiosity, they will pick your pockets clean. I know, because it has happened to me more than once.

Preparing for Your Return Trip

It is the last night of your trip, and your eyes glaze over when you think about packing for your return trip with all of your new purchases. Take my advice: Do not wait until the last night to pack. Instead, two days before, spread out all of your things and get them in order. Gather together your return tickets and necessary documents, along with credit cards and left-over cash. Place your travel clothing in another pile. Wrap fragile purchases in bubble wrap, and pack everything into your luggage. If you should discover that the zipper or wheels on your bag are broken, you will have time to remedy the situation.

Mary's Travel Gems

With businesspeople traveling the globe these days, many companies now provide short-term cell phone rentals, since your own cell phone won't work overseas. A cell phone lets you stay in touch with loved ones, make emergency calls, and even call ahead for dinner and theatre reservations. The service is surprisingly cheap! This is a super way to stay safe while traveling abroad. Find dozens of companies by typing "international cell phone rental" into Google.   ✧✧✧

If you have any old clothes or shoes you can part with, now is the time. I sometimes pack old things for this very purpose. Out with the old, in with the new.

Now you are ready to thoroughly enjoy the last day and night of your vacation without anxiety.

5
The New Millennium Travel Agent
What They Do, and Why You Still Need Them

New technology has made certain goods and services obsolete, and changed the importance of others. In the Information Age, an ordinary person with a moderate amount of computer literacy can make flight and hotel reservations anywhere in the world while wearing pajamas. That same person can delve deeply into the culture and attractions of far and exotic lands without ever having to step outside the home. The internet is an amazing resource.

However, while the worldwide web offers so much in the way of travel information, I wonder sometimes if it offers *too* much. How do you sift through all that information? How do you prioritize which sources are reliable and which are not? Have you ever had the experience of trying to find the best deal on round-trip plane tickets, only to find that by changing your departure time by an hour, or by switching to another nearby airport, your fare varied by several hundred dollars, or total travel time on one itinerary was two to three hours longer than another? Have you ever visited one of the big online travel sites to research a hotel, only to find that it has no vacancies, then gone to another website and discovered that rooms are still available? Frustrating!

The main issue here is that the internet does not allow you to type in, "I'd really like to have…," and then imaginatively accommodate your preferences and needs.

How much time did you really save by doing it yourself? How long did you spend researching and setting up your trip? One hour? Two hours or more? Do you often get a nagging feeling, after you have clicked on the "Purchase Now" button, that there is still a better deal out there, somewhere, if you could only find it?

That is the problem with the internet. There is so much information available, in so many different forms, that you can never be certain you are getting the cheapest, most convenient, shortest flights, or the best selection of hotel rooms or rental cars. If you are planning a trip to a foreign country, there is also the matter of having to research the latest health advisories, political advisories, and recent changes in document requirements. What is the safest way to get to your hotel from a foreign airport where you do not speak the language? Can you be certain you have thought of absolutely everything?

Enter the travel agent. During the dotcom bubble, travel sites on the internet burgeoned, and for a couple of years consumers had a raging love affair with being their own travel agent. But lately, they are starting to realize that travel agents are neither obsolete nor unimportant. In fact, as our lives get busier, "Time is money" is a mantra that buzzes in our ears as constantly as the low hum of our computers. That is when travel agents become indispensable.

I have said it before, but it bears repeating here: Whom do you think travelers called on September 11, 2001, when getting through to the airlines was impossible for stranded travelers? Travel agents were unsung heroes that day.

Who Needs Travel Agents?

If you need to book a round-trip flight to Florida to visit your aging Aunt Millie, chances are you can do it yourself quickly and efficiently via the internet. Travel agents are godsends, however, if you fall into one of the following categories: a frequent business traveler who needs last-minute flights to seal time-sensitive deals; a traveler whose trip involves several different legs; a person booking a specialty vacation, such as an adventure, educational, or hobby trip; an elderly, disabled, or handicapped person requiring special diet, seating, accommodations, or arrangements; a vacationer going to an unfamiliar destination who wants to get the most out of the experience; a group such as a family reunion or members of an organization wanting to travel together; or anyone who wants to save money.

Yes, I said that: *save money*. Travel agents now charge a small booking fee, usually $25 to $35. But a good travel agent knows, for instance, that fares will be going down tomorrow, or that a certain airline has specials out of a nearby, underused airport. A good travel agent can save you money by dealing directly with hotel and airline ticket consolidators—or wholesalers—who sell the same rooms and flights cheaper to travel agents than they do to the average consumer. A good travel agent stays abreast of sales, specials, and deals that ordinary people with busy lives are unlikely to discover.

Travel agents get paid commissions by airlines, hotels, rental car companies, tour companies, cruise companies, travel insurers, and others. This money does not come out of your pocket. A really great travel agent with whom you have established a relationship will jump through hoops for your repeat business, doing unsolicited research and legwork on your trip using resources you do not have access to, mining years of experience that you cannot match.

Use It or Lose It?

Don't you just hate that small print on your ticket that says your ticket is nonrefundable, no ifs, ands, or buts about it? Travel agents have found some wiggle room and loopholes in this "use it or lose it" rule. If you booked such a ticket through a travel agent and then had to cancel your trip, your travel agent might negotiate with the airline so you do not have to throw that money away. If you booked the ticket yourself, you will probably be out of luck.

What Travel Agents Do

I was recently talking to a journalist who asked me, "What, exactly, do travel agents do?" The question took me by surprise at first. But it got me thinking about how our relationship with the internet has given many people the impression that travel agents no longer provide necessary services.

Nothing could be further from the truth. In fact, when the brick-and-mortar travel agency industry was pummeled initially by online travel booking sites, it did what all smart businesses do: It did some soul searching, and then figured out how to survive and thrive by reinventing itself. Travel agents today are providers of more and better information than ever before, customized for every type of client, to ensure successful travel experiences every time.

Travel agents today are not merely booking agents. They are *destination specialists*. They have all the information about your destination at their fingertips. Chances are, they or one of their colleagues have also been there and have firsthand information to share. As destination specialists, travel agents can help you plan a trip within your budget, including airfare, hotels, and any mode of ground transportation. They can even perform such services as securing dinner reservations or setting up an appointment with a personal shopper. They take all of the guesswork out of your trip so you will feel safe and secure and can fully enjoy yourself.

They can offer you a spectrum of options, from do-it-yourself sight-seeing guides to guided tours. They have brochures and resources on every possible diversion at your destination. If you have special requests, such as wanting to find an Episcopal Church or a vegan restaurant nearby, they can nail those down for you too.

Most important, from a safety and security point of view, travel agents offer a level of protection that is hard to come by if you do it yourself. They know the laws and customs of the locals, are up on the most recent health advisories and political climate, and will not let you get on that plane, train, or ship before you have all the proper documentation. They can offer straight talk on such things as travel insurance and immunizations, and can provide you with the necessary hospital and medical clinic phone numbers and addresses at your destination. (See the Appendix for more details.)

If something should happen to you while you travel—say, you get pickpocketed, become ill, or lose your luggage—your travel agent will be your fiercest ally. Because travel agents sell the products and services for hotels, airlines, cruises, rental car companies, and tour companies, they have a lot more clout than you do for resolving disputes and extracting you from jams.

Travel agents offer years of experience that a typical consumer simply cannot acquire. I believe that today, more than ever, using a travel agent is the best way to protect yourself from unpleasant and unexpected circumstances when you are away from home.

> **Have you been scammed?**
>
> According to the National Association of Attorneys General, travel scams cost consumers $12 billion each year.

T hree days into a ten-day southern Caribbean cruise on which I was doing business and lecturing, I received an urgent phone call in my stateroom following dinner. My husband had suffered a near fatal accident and was in critical care. Could I fly there immediately? Right away, I called my travel agent in our hometown. Within an hour, she had secured all of the air transportation connections for me to fly off the coast of South America, making three connections to arrive the following evening at his bedside. I could not have relied on the cruise ship personnel to make such precise and timely arrangements. I made it to his side within twenty-four hours, which no doubt helped him make a full recovery.

How to Find a Good Travel Agent

Referrals from satisfied friends and relatives are the best way to find a great travel agent. Like other professionals whose service you trust, travel agents tend to get a lot of business through word of mouth. If your friend had a satisfying experience with one, chances are you will too.

Here are some other considerations.

Training and Experience

Travel agents are salespeople, and the products they sell are the services of the travel, hospitality, and tourism industries. To learn their trade, travel agents usually attend vocational training anywhere from six months to two years. This training is offered through community colleges or through hospitality and tourism programs in some four-year colleges. During training, prospective travel agents learn basic skills of selling travel, which involves mastering geography, learning about the various products (cruises, tours, hotels, transportation modes, etc.), becoming educated about destinations, and fine-tuning their knowledge in such areas as sightseeing, specialty travel needs, and safety and security issues.

Because there is no national accreditation for travel agents—and therefore no good way to police the industry in a uniform way—I always recommend that you find a travel agent who has at least four years experience. If the travel agency is a storefront operation, ask them how long they have been in business. In most states, travel sellers have to be licensed and registered under the state's travel promotion laws. Contact your state's department of consumer affairs to find out how and if your state regulates travel agents.

Knowledge and Expertise

You can tell very quickly how well your travel agent knows her stuff. Travel agents get swamped with information in the form of magazines, articles, emails, industry updates, travel advisories, and so on. A good travel agent is a voracious reader, learner, and a frequent traveler.

Always ask your travel agent if she has been to your destination. One reason people go into this vocation is the travel perks. Travel agents love to travel, and they get paid to do so by tourist boards of governments, hotels and resorts, and by cruises, who invite them to sample their offerings for free or at a steep discount (which the travel agent can write off as a business expense). If your travel agent has been in the business for a few years, there is an excellent chance she will have been to your destination, or someone in her office has been there. If not, she has probably attended a seminar or lecture to get educated about it.

Perks, Perks, Perks

Women account for 87 percent of all travel agents. The average travel agent makes around $26,000 a year base salary, and travel agency managers make about $33,000. However, once you add on commissions and loads of tax-deductible free travel, not to mention vacations and other benefits, travel agents can earn six figures.

Source: www. astanet.com

A few years ago, we were selling a lot of trips to Hawaii and they advertised packages for $399, which included airfare and hotel in Honolulu. We had an inside joke in our agency about this package, which we avoided like the plague, despite its cheap price tag for our customers. This hotel was in such a bad part of town that there were several rapes and tons of other problems, and everyone in the industry knew about its reputation. I would delicately steer my customers elsewhere, advising them to pay the extra $200 for the week and stay in a safe and reputable place instead. The bargain offering went on for some time, and I have often thought of the unsuspecting travelers who sacrificed their safety to save a few bucks.

Specialty Travel Specialists

Because the travel industry is consumer driven, travel agents are super-responsive to special requests and special needs. Specialty or lifestyle travel is one of the fastest growing sectors of the industry right now. This includes everything from trips and tours that cater to handicapped, disabled, or elderly consumers, to extreme adventure or niche-hobby themed vacations.

If you want to book a vacation that involves out-of-the-ordinary services or activities, doing so through a travel agent is an absolute must, in my opinion. I cannot tell you how disconcerting it is to be in a place like Israel and meet well-meaning priests or religious leaders directing a group on a religious pilgrimage—yet the leader has never been there before and is not educated about the specific offerings and security issues of that area. When you book specialty travel, the idea is to get the most out of your time and money. Do not try to do it yourself. Not only might you end up in an unsavory hotel or area, but you might miss some of the greatest attractions of your destination. A travel agent gives you the best bang for your travel buck, and will make certain that your trip is enjoyable and safe too.

Travel Agent Dos and Don'ts

Do:

- Shop around until you find a travel agent with whom you feel comfortable. Stop in at the mall and chat with a storefront travel agent or call local travel agents on the phone. Ask friends whom they used and what kind of experience they had before and during their trip.

- Come to the travel agent with a budget in mind. Never show up with a vague sense of how much you want to spend. Providing your travel agent with budget parameters will help her make the best possible arrangements you can afford.

- Ask the travel agent if she has personally been to the destination. Firsthand travel experience is the travel agent's most prized asset. Be sure to use one who has either traveled to your destination or is well educated about it. A good travel agent will be honest with you and might recommend a colleague who has been there.
- Ask the travel agent why she is recommending a certain hotel, rental car company, cruise line, etc. Her answer should reflect value: price plus quality. Aggressive selling of a product that you are not interested in is a bad sign.
- Come prepared with a list of questions for the travel agent about: required documentation, health advisories, political advisories, safety precautions, sights, attractions, local customs, currency, etc. Do not be shy about calling afterwards if you have more questions.
- Ask your travel agent what booking fees she is charging you. If it is an exorbitant amount of money, you are dealing with the wrong person.

Don't:

- Go into a travel agent and say, "I want to go on a vacation. What do you suggest?" Make a list of the kinds of activities, hobbies, sights, food, and entertainment you are interested in beforehand. With some basic guidelines from you, your travel agent will be able to arrange a vacation that suits your temperament, preferences, and budget.
- Stay with a travel agent with whom you do not feel a personal affinity. If you want a dynamic relationship with a travel agent who is intuitive about your needs and understands what you want, then it is imperative that you like her and that the two of you get along.

- Hide special needs from your travel agent, such as diet or medical requirements, or preferences, such as gay travel. She wants you to have the best trip possible so you will become a loyal, repeat customer. Let her do the work for you; do not omit out-of-the-ordinary requests from your dialogue.
- Waste a travel agent's time if you are not serious about taking a trip. Remember that your travel agent is paid by commissions, so you would be, in essence, asking her to work for free. Would you be willing to do that for someone?

Now, More than Ever

On September 11, 2001, Americans had an awful wake-up call. When it comes to travel, no longer is ignorance bliss. It is more important now to do detailed planning of your trip than it has been in the past. Using a travel agent takes much of the guesswork out of your trip and increases the safety factor by a wide margin. You will not be standing around in a strange city trying to figure out how to get to the hotel while opportunistic people observe your vulnerability. You will not end up in an unsafe area of town. And you will not find yourself stranded by unforeseen circumstances trying to figure out on your own what to do next. Your travel agent back home is standing by to make calls, book new connections, and advocate for you in any unexpected situation. Now more than ever, using a travel agent makes the best sense from a safety and security point of view.

6
Top Tips for Traveling Solo

There are 82 million unmarried adults in the United States, or 40 percent of the adult population in the nation. Of all women sixty-five or older, 55.7 percent are single—never married, divorced, or widowed. And one-third of our total population are baby-boomers—people born between 1946 and 1964—the prime age range for traveling.

You would think the American travel industry would be jumping through hoops to serve this enormous market of potential travelers. Quite the opposite is true! A single person who books hotel rooms, cruises, and tours, for example, will be charged for the extra bed she did not sleep in and the extra towels she did not use. Tour operators and travel companies continue to force single travelers to share hotel rooms, or face paying 50 to 150 percent more for the luxury of having their own rooms. Major tour and cruise companies are beginning to change their singles policies, but not soon enough. For example, most cruise lines charge 25 to 100 percent extra for solo travelers who request a stateroom that could be a double-person cabin.

> **Going It Alone**
>
> According to the recent American Traveler's Survey, conducted by Plog Research Group, 27.5% of the U.S. population traveled solo on their last vacation.

Europe, on the other hand, caters to solo travelers. European hotels commonly offer single rooms at single rates. It is extremely normal in Europe to see people dining, sightseeing, and traveling alone.

Traveling single is a specialty of mine as well as the subject of a popular seminar I conduct entitled "Traveling Single in a Doubles World." Taking trips on your own brings unique challenges and rewards. Here are my top tips for protecting yourself when you are traveling alone.

Cappuccinos, Xerox, and Me

One of my favorite things to do is to go to the local bookstore, grab a stack of travel guides, and sit down in the café area with a cappuccino. I bring along sticky tabs and mark pages that have great travel resources for singles. Then I meander over to the photocopier and make copies of those pages to file in my travel scrapbook for later.

✈ **Do your homework ahead of time.** Make a scrapbook. Take notes from newspapers and magazines, print out web pages, and photocopy pages from travel books about restaurants, local sightseeing tours, and great places to stay when going it alone. There are oodles of resources out there for single travelers. Organizations that specialize in singles travel are great "ideas" places. Particularly singles-friendly are organizations specializing in educational, adventure, ecotourism, and expedition trips. Be on the lookout for inexpensive, offbeat accommodations such as convents, universities, single tents, and shared cabins that cater to the person traveling alone. Doing your own research will help you avoid hassles and misunderstandings when you are ready to fine-tune and book your trip.

✈ **When it comes to traveling solo, be a savvy consumer.** Learn to ask the right questions and you will find the best deals. When browsing travel brochures and ads, read the fine print and look for such phrases as "based on double occupancy." Singles do not pay half the double rate.

Instead, they pay half that rate plus a supplement. Call hotels and ask if they have special promotional rates. Travel agents can be helpful here. Have your travel agent find you a hotel that charges the lowest singles supplement. For travel in Europe, your travel agent should be able to find a small room exclusively for singles at a special rate in one of the older hotels. Ask about flexible singles-only packages that let you in on group-tour rates by sharing meals, for example, without having to participate in all of the group's activities. Occasionally, a tour packager will not charge a singles supplement at all if, for example, the trip has not sold out. And there are lots of ways to save if you do not mind doubling up with another traveler. To help clients save money and gain companionship (though not necessarily romance), many firms catering to singles offer to pair you up with a roommate based on age, smoking preference, and other criteria. See the Appendix for these and other sources.

✈ Learn some basic verbal and nonverbal communication skills.
Every country has unfamiliar customs and taboos. In addition to learning some basic phrases of the native language, it is essential to familiarize yourself with local ways. An American woman travel-

---

Advantages of Traveling Solo

- Total control
- Trip designed just for you
- No distractions or having to be responsible for another
- Element of surprise
- Self-discovery, self-reliance
- Builds character: I can do it!
- Develops social skills and openness to others
- Magical discoveries through "your eyes only"

Disadvantages of Traveling Solo

- Often paying more
- Finding places to dine
- Transfer and transiting from point to point
- Unruly luggage
- Not being able to share experiences in the moment
- Having every moment filled and fulfilled
- Being perceived as a target by criminals

ing alone, for example, should know how to dress properly in predominantly Muslim countries. Men and women should understand local taboos and implied meaning behind socializing with the opposite sex, as well as what is generally considered socially acceptable in terms of gay and lesbian associations. Even if romance is not on your travel agenda, it is a good idea to know the social and legal parameters beforehand.

✈ **Give travel information to a trusted person at home.** Leave a copy of your personal documents (credit card information, passport and visa, medical information, insurance information); itinerary; hotel information (email, address, phone numbers); cell phone number; and other details about your trip with a trusted person back home for safekeeping. Leave the same with your travel agent.

✈ **Establish "check-in" appointments with friends or relatives back home.** Work out an easy-to-accomplish, predetermined time to contact a friend or relative back home. I have found that traveling alone is a bit like being a teenager again. No matter how old we are and no matter how much we love our newfound freedom, there is a part of us that needs to know someone at home is looking out for our well-being and expecting our call or email at a specific time. Making an appointment to call a loved one keeps me "grounded" while I am off having adventures halfway around the globe. If you were to get into some kind of danger or trouble while traveling alone, there would be someone at home who could notify authorities when you failed to "check in." Virtually anywhere in the world, you

---

Destinations I Avoid

n my own experience traveling alone, I have found the following destinations particularly unfriendly or dangerous:

- Africa (all parts, except Egypt)
- Balkan region (former Yugoslavia)
- Store parking lots (at night)
- Washington, D.C.
- Philippines
- Indonesia
- Brazil
- Areas of the Middle East
- Areas of Asia

can find an internet café to keep in touch with your family and friends back home.

✈ **Pack lightly.** One of my favorite things about traveling by myself is feeling free and unencumbered. Do not complicate your travel by lugging around heavy bags and gear. Keep it as simple as possible by bringing only the bare necessities with you. You will end up having a more successful trip if you have fewer possessions to store and worry about.

✈ **Wear clothing and shoes that are comfortable and conservative.** Wear shoes you can run in. Dress to blend in. Keep your hands free by wearing a money belt (containing money, credit cards, documents, and emergency information) under loose-fitting clothing, and use a daypack, fanny pack, or traveler's vest to hold other items such as tissues, camera, and cell phone for easy accessibility. Do not wear jewelry or expensive watches.

✈ **Choose a hotel in a good location.** This will be *your* neighborhood for the duration of your trip, so pick a safe one. Find a hotel that has a restaurant or café on premises, or an eatery nearby that is open late. Make sure there are good transportation options close by.

✈ **Make your hotel accommodations safe and secure.** When you arrive at your hotel, do not announce that you are traveling alone. Always ask for the safest room possible—not one that is on the first floor or next to an outdoor fire escape or roof ladder, for

In-room Bathrooms

Having your own private bathroom, especially if you are elderly or traveling alone, makes a huge difference in your comfort level. Always ask the hotel clerk for a room that has an in-room bathroom. In older and smaller hotels in Europe, bathrooms and washrooms are sometimes down the hall, and this may be unavoidable.

example. Tell the hotel clerk to write down or whisper the number of your room. Have him or her swipe your card twice to be sure another card is not activated. Use the hotel vault—not the in-room hotel safe—to store any valuables. Always keep your room door latched from the inside. Never open your door to a stranger or order food from a local carryout joint such as a Chinese restaurant or pizza shop. Never enter your room when some-one is out in the hallway. Always use the elevator, not the stairs, if you have a choice. And do not get into the elevator if you do not like the look or feel of a fellow passenger. Leave the "Do Not Disturb" sign on your door if you do not want hotel workers entering your room. Never leave your room-service tray outside in the hallway. This could tell passersby that the occupant ordered a meal for one and is probably alone.

✈ **Know where you are going.** Wandering around in a foreign city can be lots of fun, but it is a good idea to chat with the concierge or hotel clerk before you set off. Ask him or her for directions and advice. Buy a detailed street map and a highlighter and have the concierge mark the way for you. Also, ask him or her to write the directions in English and in the native lan-guage. If you will be traveling by taxi, ask the doorman to tell the driver where you are going. Always keep a postcard of your hotel with address and phone number in your money belt. If you get lost, do not worry. I have found that people are amazingly friendly and helpful all over the world. If you feel more comfortable with asking directions from a family, seek one out instead of walking up to the first stranger. Never tell a stranger that you are lost or that you are alone. And never, ever get in a car with a stranger.

✈ **Take advantage of local guides.** One of the best ways to see a city when you are traveling solo is with a local driver or local guide. When I am in a new destination and want to do some sightseeing or shopping, I check out local sightseeing companies and book a guide for a half day. These are trained professionals who really know their turf. In my experience, they are usually great people who are willing to take me anyplace, drive me wherever I want to go, and go out of their way to help me have a great experience. When I find a particularly wonderful taxi driver in a foreign city, I sometimes ask him if he would be willing to take me around the following day, or come back two hours later to pick me up. Most foreign cabbies are not like those in New York City whom you might never see again—and would not want to, anyway! The foreign taxi drivers I have met take a personal interest in my comfort and safety—fabulous local resources for the solo traveler. Ask them to take you to their favorite restaurants. What could be a better way to get the local flavor, literally?

✦ **Practice behavioral self-defense.** What do I mean by this? I am talking about universal body language. Use eye contact carefully. It is okay to ignore people or to look away. In many parts of the world, prolonged, direct eye contact is considered provocative. If you get an odd feeling about your driver while riding in a taxi, pull out your cell phone and pretend to call someone local. As I have recommended before, learn a few words in the native tongue, even if you do not understand the response. Being able to ask for something in their language sends a subtle message that you know what you are doing and are not helpless.

> **4 Things to Save Your Life**
>
> 1. American money, to bribe your captors or pay off your rescuer
> 2. Note pad and pencil, to get your message across with stick figures
> 3. Cell phone and local emergency numbers
> 4. Mini flashlight

✦ **Be your own best friend.** It is easy when you travel alone to get overtired, to let your mind wander, to get lonely, or to drink a little too much alcohol. Remember that you do not have a friend along to help you out of a pinch. Be your own best friend. Consciously remind yourself to drink in moderation. And never, ever leave your drink unattended. Be very, very careful about whom you invite to your table or back to your hotel room. He or she may be someone you cannot shake. Do not give out too much personal information. One way to enhance your experience when traveling alone is to keep a journal or scrapbook. Take pictures, collect postcards, and jot down thoughts and impressions. It is a great way to spend time, feel productive, and fend off loneliness.

7
Top Tips for Traveling with Children

Family travel is booming, and experts predict this trend will continue to gain momentum during the next decade. One reason for this is that frequent flyer miles have enabled whole families to take vacations by plane. Another is that travel companies are now catering to families by offering soft adventure, educational, and nature-oriented vacations, specifically designed with youngsters in mind. The net effect is that the world is getting smaller for families, and the travel industry is responding in kind with child-oriented amenities.

In terms of health and safety when traveling with children, the two most challenging aspects are the stress factor (yours and theirs), and keeping track of them. In some ways, traveling with children forces us to be more vigilant, more aware, and better prepared than we would be just for ourselves. It is simple reality of parenting that bringing kids along forces us to allow extra time, for example, or to think about when the next meal or snack will be. (Every parent knows as soon as everyone is buckled up, one of the children will declare, "I'm hungry!")

> **Please, Can We Go There?**
>
> According to a recent survey, 57% of 1,600 adults who responded said that children were influential in selecting destinations. Children aged 2 to 14 influenced $188 billion in parental travel-related spending.
>
> Source: Nat'l Leisure Travel Monitor

We tend to anticipate and pay attention to their needs more than we do our own.

I have divided this chapter into two parts. First, I list my top tips for getting the most out of family trips, whether traveling with toddlers or teens. Next, I include my top tips for children traveling alone.

✈ Take care of legal and medical requirements ahead of time. If only one parent is traveling outside the country with children, you will be required to have a notarized letter from the other biological parent giving permission for the child to leave the United States. Airlines will not make any concessions if you do not have this letter. Canada and Mexico are particularly strict, even if you are just driving across the border to shop. Also, make certain your child's (and your own) immunizations are up to date.

✈ Organize the child's documents. Put together a packet that includes a copy of the itinerary, the child's passport, medical insurance numbers, immunization records, list of allergies, your cell phone number, hotel address and phone number where you will be staying, contact person back home, and legal letter of permission from the other parent, if necessary (see

above). Your child should have one set of these in a money belt, and one set should be kept with your documents. If anything were to happen to you, or if you got separated from the child, you could feel confident that your child would be all right. By the way, never put a nametag on the outside of your child's clothing or bags where unscrupulous strangers might read them.

✈ **Book the right seat.** When traveling with children, good seats can make a big difference in everyone's comfort on a long trip. First-row, economy class is the best seat to reserve on a plane if you can; it has lots of leg and play room. Children under the age of fifteen are not permitted in an exit row seat. If you are traveling with an infant with a child-restraint seat, you are not permitted to book any of the following: emergency exit rows or the row directly forward or aft of an emergency exit row; aisle seats; or bulkhead seats when the car seat is a combination car seat and stroller.

> ### Flying with an Infant?
>
> Two little known facts about flying with babies:
>
> (1) If your infant is less than two weeks old, the airline may require a physician's written approval to fly.
>
> (2) Do not assume you can bring your own baby seat on the plane. The only child-restraint seats allowed onboard are those that meet FAA guidelines.

✈ **Talk about airport security with your kids.** It is a good idea to prepare children for security checkpoints. Make sure they do not have toy guns or other toy weapons in their carry-on luggage. Remember that even tiny child's scissors used for craft projects will be confiscated. And remind them not to joke about bombs, guns, and terrorism.

✈ **Pack a child's carry-on roller bag full of activities.** The key to stress-free travel with little ones is keeping them busy, busy, busy. The same goes for teens. The main contents of your child's wheeled carry-on bag, besides a familiar blanket or stuffed animal and some overnight essentials in case checked-through luggage gets lost, should be books, toys, games, art supplies, tiny tubs of play dough or modeling clay, puzzles, mazes, tiny magnetized travel board games, computerized toys, a blank journal, stationery, craft projects, and a disposable camera. Assume the worst—that you will be stranded in an airport overnight, or that your child will get sick and be stuck in your hotel room for days on end. Then prepare. I guarantee that having dozens of games and projects will make everyone happier—on the trip, in restaurants, in the hotel when you want to sleep late, and so on. Do not forget that teenagers like games too!

> ## Protecting Little Ears on Planes
>
> Children's ears tend to be more sensitive than adults' to changes in airplane cabin pressure when landing and taking off. Here are some tried-and-true tricks:
>
> • Practice pretend yawns.
>
> • Chew gum.
>
> • Suck on a lollipop.
>
> • Sip water.
>
> • Give babies a bottle.
>
> • Give babies a pacifier.

✈ **Do not let them get hungry or thirsty.** Whether in transit or when sightseeing, always keep water and healthy snacks handy. Again, assume the worst—that you could be stuck on the plane sitting on a runway for six hours. Keeping kids happy improves the travel experience for them, you, and those around you.

✈ **Rehearse "what if" scenarios.** When was the last time you went over with your child what to do if he or she were approached by a stranger? Review the basic rules. Talk about and make plans for where to meet and what to do if your child gets separated from you. Designate a meeting place at each site you visit while traveling. Create a family whistle or call, something your child could readily identify in a crowd. Bring along walkie-talkies, preferably expensive models that have a two- to four-mile range. Practice using it in your hotel until your child can operate it masterfully. Never go anywhere without your cell phone number and hotel number and address tucked inside a money belt worn by your child.

✈ **Turn one activity into a daily routine.** For children, the most stressful part of traveling is lack of routine. Adventure, excitement, and new experiences are great, but kids also need to feel grounded. One of the best ways to do this is to plan quiet, reflective time each day, either in the morning or in the afternoon, to write letters or postcards back home, or to work on a travel journal or scrapbook. (These will become treasured mementos later in life.) Be sure to pack a notebook, glue stick and tape, scissors (in your checked-through luggage), and colored markers or pencils, as well as stationery. Little ones can cut out the pictures from postcards and sightseeing brochures for their scrapbook. New words and phrases, as well as their observations about new foods, customs, and styles of dress, make great scrapbook and journal entries. Let children take their own photographs. If you have an active child, plan a daily exercise regimen.

> ### Mary's Travel Gems
>
> Many hotels have VCRs in the room. For downtime, nothing beats watching a favorite movie. This can also give you extra time in the morning for sleeping late if your children wake up too early. ❖❖❖

✈ **Teach them to be alert.** I have found that children, interestingly, tend to be more alert, more intuitive, and more sensitive to danger, odd characters, or suspicious activity than their supposedly savvy and experienced parents. If a child points out a stranger who seems "weird" or "creepy," pay attention. Often children pick up on things we grown-ups have become too jaded to notice. Teach children to be wary of sudden commotions in crowds—the favorite pickpocketer's technique. If you are in a European city where gypsies live, remind children that these colorful and exotic people are often professional thieves, and to stay close to adults when they swarm up to you.

Children Traveling Alone

More children are traveling unaccompanied by adults than ever before, and the age of these solo travelers is getting younger. Most of this is due to the rising divorce rate, with children having to shuttle between two households, often in different states. Another trend, however, is teen travel. We have all heard about teenagers flying down en masse to Cancun for Spring Break, unheard of just twenty years ago. Additionally, high schoolers now trade the traditional summer camp experience for exotic educational trips that look good on college applications—language and culture immersion, art or music courses, research projects, service-oriented internships—that often take place halfway across the globe.

All of this has raised concern on the part of the travel industry, which has responded with a slew of updated regulations.

Regulations for Unaccompanied Minors

Every airline has slightly different rules and rates regarding children flying alone, and these vary for domestic versus international flights as well. It is best to have your travel agent or an airline employee give you a copy of the complete regulations. Some general airline industry rules follow:

- No child under the age of five may travel unaccompanied. A child under five may be accompanied by a companion traveler as young as twelve, or by a paid airline escort.
- A parent or guardian must accompany children aged five to twelve until they are aboard the airplane, and should remain in the gate area until the plane takes off.
- For children aged five to twelve, you must arrange unaccompanied minor service (UM Service) from the airline ahead of time.

Teach Johnny to Speak

If you are traveling abroad, teaching your child a few basic phrases in the native language is fun, rewarding, and most of all, smart. Practice asking for help and directions in a different language.

What Unaccompanied Minor Service Does not Include

- Administering of medications
- In-flight entertainment
- Waiting at destination for the pick-up adult
- Arranging for ground transportation upon arrival

The cost of UM Service varies from airline to airline, but ranges from $30 to $100 per flight. Full UM Service may also be requested for children twelve to seventeen. UM Service includes some or all of the following, depending on the airline: airport terminal assistance in making connecting flights and going through security, holding of travel documents for safekeeping, helping the child on and off the plane. The escort is not always a single person. Often the "escort" is multiple employees, each taking charge of one part of the journey and handing off the child at connection points.

- Most airlines will only accept unaccompanied children under eight if the flight is nonstop. Most airlines have other flight restrictions, such as flight time and destinations. For example, an airline will not book an unaccompanied minor on the last connecting flight of a given evening to avoid the possibility of the child having to spend the night in a hotel. If bad weather threatens, the airline may rebook the child on an alternate flight.
- Each airline has specific drop-off and pick-up requirements for children traveling alone. Usually, the airline requires identification and proof of age for the child; the name, address, and telephone number of the pick-up adult; and requires the pickup adult to have proof of identity and to sign a release for the child upon pick-up.
- Children must wear an "Unaccompanied Minor" identification tag at all times.

Top Tips for Children Traveling Alone

✦ **Get the scoop ahead of time.** Ask your travel agent or the airline to provide you with the airline's policies for children traveling alone. Ask if you need special documentation, such as a notarized letter giving permission for the child to travel alone. Ask if children's meals are available. And do not be shy about requesting special kids' promotions or rates. Be prepared to pay more for Unaccompanied Minor Service on each flight. Make a duplicate copy of the pertinent regulations for the pick-up adult, and review them thoroughly so he or she knows where to be, at what time, and what documents to have on hand.

✦ **Think of the child's comfort.** Book a window seat so the child can look out on take-off and landing and has a comfy place to lean against for naps. Try to book a seat near the galley so flight attendants can keep an eye on your child, and so the child will be able to readily ask for help if needed. Pack—overpack—toys, games, books, activities, and small projects so your child will not feel lonely or bored. A favorite doll, blanket, or toy is a good idea. Also, pack plenty of water, healthy snacks, and edible goodies. Tiny wrapped surprises are good ways to fend off fear.

✈ **Turn your child into a savvy traveler and an expert.** Review all drop-off and pick-up arrangements thoroughly with your child so he or she will not be in the dark and will feel confident and safe. Make sure the child zips emergency numbers, ID, and cash into a kid-friendly money belt, sock wallet, or fanny pouch. Remind your child to stay with the assigned airline staff at all times while in airports, especially when going into a public washroom. Tell him or her to stay buckled at all times while seated. Instruct your child not to reveal travel arrangements, name, or any other personal information to strangers. Go over basic rules of etiquette, such as using good manners while eating, using the call button very sparingly, and asking politely for assistance.

✈ **Teach your child how to ask for help.** The two reasons children get into trouble are that they are too trusting and they feel insecure about asking for help. Remind your child that if she child is uncomfortable with the person sitting next to her, she has the right to ask for a new seat. Teach your child how to remain calm but insistent if she senses trouble and needs help. Role-play some situations—preferably annoying ones, not scary ones—so she can practice asking for help.

> **My Tiny Bubbles**
>
> I always carry a tiny bubble flask, about the size of a lipstick, in my pocket. You can buy these at dollar stores or toyshops. When I am on a plane and a child in front of me is miserable, rambunctious, or downright ornery, I get out my tiny wand and blow a few bubbles over to the child. It works like a charm to calm them down and change their mood.

✈ **Give your child a prepaid calling card.** And then show him how to use it. There is nothing quite as comforting to a child or a teenager as knowing that Mom or Dad is just a phone call away. It also gives him a sense of responsibility to know that you expect a call. If possible, have the child call you as soon as he arrives at his destination.

8
Top Tips for Business Travel

How is a business traveler different from a leisure traveler? Business travelers are frequent travelers. They are used to traveling on relatively short notice. And their trips are shorter and have to be better organized. As I have mentioned before, if we would plan *every* trip like a business trip, traveling would be safer, easier, and more pleasant all around.

Because of their compressed schedules and specific meeting times, business travelers are more affected by delays, lost luggage, illness, poor connections, and car and hotel foul-ups than are leisure travelers. That is the bad news. The good news is that business travelers tend to be targeted less by petty thieves and criminals, probably because they are focused and on-schedule, rather than wide-eyed and unguarded, as tourists tend to be.

> **Wake Me Up**
>
> If you have an appointment you cannot afford to miss, bring your own alarm clock. Hotel wake-up services and hotel alarm clocks are not always reliable.

Below are my top tips to help ensure that your next business trip is safe, trouble-free, and healthy.

✈ **Use a travel agent specializing in business travel.** Travel agents who cater to business travelers specialize in airlines, hotels, and cars. They know the best, fastest, and cheapest way to get there, and are familiar with the hotel amenities you require for working, conferencing, dining on the run, meetings, fax and internet hookup in your room, and so on. It used to be that businesses would simply pick up the air and hotel tab, no matter the price. But now businesses are cutting back on travel or looking for the best deals, which has left airlines and hotels fighting for business clients. Find a travel agent who stays abreast of the latest business-related developments in the industry, and then stick with her.

✈ **Avoid end-of-trip gotchas.** The success of a business trip smells less sweet once you get home and find out that you have to foot much of the bill. Thoroughly review and understand your company's travel policy before you leave on your first trip, and keep a copy of that agreement with you. You should be crystal clear about which expenses are covered and which you are expected to pick up on your own.

✈ **Insure your trip.** For business trips, travel insurance is an absolute necessity. Internationally is it even more critical, because frequent flights are not available in case your flight would be cancelled because of bad weather. Verify that your business is paying for both travel insurance, which will cover the expense of last-minute rebooking, and car rental insurance. If you upgrade to an SUV, convertible, or other model, find out if the insurance covers the upgraded model. It may not.

✈ **Minimize transportation times.** Book a hotel in a convenient location. Minimizing shuttle time and distance between meetings ultimately adds to your safety. Look at your meetings agenda. Where and when is your first and last meeting? Will you be entertaining clients at your hotel? At what time is your departing flight? I usually book a hotel near my meetings, but if I have a very early morning flight out, I might book a room by the airport instead. Weigh these variables to find the option that is most practical and the least stressful. Next, know ahead of time how you will get from the airport to your hotel, and how long it will take. Your travel agent or the hotel representative will be able to provide this information for you. Pick-up services are generally the best and most reliable form of ground transportation from the airport because they are right there waiting for you when your plane lands.

✈ **Do not follow the herds.** When a flight is delayed or cancelled, a planeload of disgruntled fellow passengers heads straight for the ticket counter to book alternative flights. But not you. Jot down or preprogram into your cell phone the 800 number of your airline ahead of time. Then sit in a comfy chair and call the airline. The person on the other end of the phone can, in most cases, rebook you quicker than that on-site airline employee who is being harassed by a herd of frantic passengers. While you are at it, reconfirm your hotel and car reservations. This really works!

✈ **Join the club.** Long layovers are the new reality for travelers. However, there is no need to lose a day of work just because you are traveling. Join an airline club or have your business buy you a membership. For the business traveler, it is so much better to work in a quiet lounge on your laptop than to kill time in a busy, noisy, public waiting area. Airline clubs are a great way to ensure that you arrive refreshed and "on" for your first meeting. If your business will not spring for it, I still believe it is a worthwhile out-of-pocket expense. Here is what clubs offer: proximity to the most used gates; free snacks and beverages; television; the free use of private offices for meetings if you reserve ahead of time; and fax and internet connections. The best thing clubs offer: peace and quite time.

✈ **Be comfortable en route.** Make the traveling part of your business trip as easy as possible. Wear comfortable shoes and clothing. Put your briefcase and carry-on luggage on wheels so your hands remain free and your muscles do not get strained. Do some stretches on the airplane to keep your neck, shoulders, legs, and feet limber. If you have a meeting scheduled soon after arrival, I recommend wearing lightweight nylon sweats on the plane, and changing into business clothes and shoes upon landing.

✈ **Downsize.** Airlines are now reserving the right to take your carry-on bag from you and check it through if it exceeds their weight or size restrictions. Imagine the worst—that your checked-through bags will get lost—and then plan for it by carrying onboard everything you need, if possible, avoiding checked baggage altogether. Because of the new limitations, downsizing to just one medium-sized carry-on and another smaller item is more necessary than ever. For a short business trip, your main carry-on could have one business outfit, including shoes, one casual outfit, workout clothes, and prescription drugs and personal care items. The smaller carry-on item that must fit under your seat would be a briefcase with your laptop and business materials. Do you really need more?

> ### Hot Tubbing Is Risky Business
>
> Wonderful though they seem, hotel hot tubs are either breeding tanks for bacteria if heated incorrectly, or vats of toxic chemicals that kill germs. Either way, hot tubs are unhealthy. A safer way to unwind is to draw a bath full of the hottest water you can tolerate and enjoy a private spa in your room.

✈ **For foreign business trips, review cultural dos and don'ts.** Conducting business outside of our country and familiar culture can be tricky. I was once seconds away from addressing a Japanese businessman's female companion as *Missus,* had I not been grabbed by a friend in the nick of time who clued me in that she was his *mistress,* not his wife—a common practice in Japanese corporate culture! Without understanding the basic conventions such as rules of address, attire, dining manners, dietary restrictions, punctuality, and religious norms, you could unwittingly turn a positive business experience into a diplomatic nightmare. It never hurts to inform your foreign contact beforehand that you are relatively unfamiliar with his or her culture. Ask questions to clear up uncertainties. Your colleague will respect your sincerity and thoughtfulness.

✈ **Boost your brain energy.** Perhaps the most difficult thing about business travel is the need to perform at your mental peak, often as soon as you land. If you have a jam-packed schedule with little down time, here is my advice. Drink lots of water and avoid airplane food. Take a catnap on the plane if you can. If that is impossible, do some deep-breathing exercises to ease stress and to oxygenate your brain. Face, neck, and shoulder exercises along with feet, ankle, and calf stretches are ones you can do in your seat without attracting attention. I am always amazed at how small stretches make me feel relaxed, recharged, and mentally alert. If you have time between meetings, try to schedule in a brisk walk, a short work-out or swim at your hotel, or a nap or steam bath. The key here is to maximize blood flow to your brain while minimizing travel stress. If your flight offers meals, special-order the healthiest one they offer twenty-four hours in advance.

✈ **Make breakfast meetings.** If you hit it off with a business contact and want to do more networking, consider setting a breakfast meeting, rather than getting together for dinner and drinks. I have noticed that at power breakfasts, I get my colleague's full attention. Our minds are fresh and a new day is in front of us. Cocktails and expensive dinners can be fun, but if productivity is your goal, you can achieve more by using breakfasts to jump-start your day.

9

Top Tips for Lifestyle and Specialty Travel

What the heck is lifestyle and specialty travel, you ask? This is one of the fastest growing segments of the travel industry. It includes ecotourism, adventure trips, hobby-driven travel, gay travel, nude vacationing, spa hopping, pilgrimages, volunteer or work vacations, and educational travel. It also includes disability and elder travel (to which I have devoted a separate chapter).

Today, people want more out of their vacation than to loll on the beach and read a book. *They want to have a learning and growing experience.* They want to enrich themselves. Perhaps you want to swim with the dolphins and do conservation work with marine biologists on the same trip. Maybe your dual love of literature and French cuisine has led you to seek out

Need Some Ideas?

It's easy to find a vacation suited to your own interests. Here are just a few examples to give you an idea of the many options out there:

- antiquing
- aromatherapy tours
- ballooning
- cave exploring
- birding
- cooking schools
- brewery hopping
- horsetrekking through Russia
- Japanese quilting
- Greek isles for lesbians
- ice climbing
- murder mystery excursions
- opera cities
- rainforest research
- Renaissance Faires
- sports tours
- supernatural and haunted places
- vegetarian lifestyle

and retrace Hemingway's culinary tour of Paris. Or you have a passion for hang gliding and want to do it in an exotic part of the world. Whether it it thrills or enlightenment you are after, you can be sure that the travel industry has already thought of it and offers the opportunity to make your dream a reality.

Lifestyle and specialty travel differs from other types of travel in that you are not merely going with the flow or setting out to relax. Rather, you are embarking on an adventure with a purpose, setting out with specific goals and expectations. On this type of trip, you often travel with people of like mind who share similar interests or lifestyles. It is fine for you to have expectations, but ensure your well-being while away from home by remembering this mantra: *Expect the unexpected.*

I would put adventure travel into three categories: soft, hard, and exploration/expedition. Soft adventure includes moderate activity such as walking, hiking, backpacking, spa hopping, and sailing. Hard adventure, a step up on the thrill-seeking ladder, would include more perilous activities, such as whitewater rafting in the Grand Canyon, weeklong kayak excursions on the high seas, and trekking in Nepal. Expedition or exploration adventures would be things like African safaris, archaeological digs in Egypt, or exploring the ancient ruins of Mexico. Depending on the level of physical challenge, keep in mind that adventure travel tends have inherent safety drawbacks that mere sightseeing does not.

> ### Your Nose Remembers
>
> If you want to enhance your vacation memory, here is something you can do besides take photographs and keep a journal. Buy an unfamiliar cologne or perfume and wear it every day of your trip. A couple of weeks after you return, splash on that scent again. Experts say you will be able to recall your trip in vivid detail.

Here are some of my top tips to make your experience safer and more rewarding.

✈ **Know your physical limitations.** If you are setting out on an adventure trip that involves a radically different climate, schedule, or more physical activity than you are accustomed to, be realistic about your abilities and health. Talk to your doctor or trainer. Do a test run beforehand, if possible, such as hiking or canoeing near where you live. Do not set unreasonable physical challenges for yourself. If you do, your trip will not be fun, and you will put yourself, and possibly others, in danger.

✈ **Know your emotional limitations.** You will be challenged psychologically as well as physically, so consider your needs. Is quiet or solitude important to you? Would you be miserable with an unpleasant roommate on a group tour? If so, spring for a single room, which may cost an extra $200 or $300. Experts have found that homesickness is extremely common among adult travelers, so bring along a comfort item from home, such as a pillow or a hot water bottle to smooth out bumpy emotional moments.

> **Homesickness: Not Just for Kids**
>
> My husband used to say he could set the clock by my first phone call home when traveling. Without fail, I would call him on my third day, sounding mopey. "Are you ready to come home?" he would ask. "Totally," I would say. After the third day, I usually settle into a groove and all is well. Experts now agree that homesickness is a common adult experience, so prepare for it.

✈ **Plan well.** If you are using a travel agent, find one with expertise in the type of travel you seek. A knowledgeable expert can tie up all loose ends and leave little to chance so that you know where you are going, whom you will be with, and for how long. As a money-saving alternative to all-inclusive tour packages, you might try booking your own airfare and hotel, and then using half-day or full-day onsite tour companies. Local universities in foreign cities offer courses and even work-study opportunities. However, if you decide to plan a trip this way, you will have to be your own travel agent and consider such details as where the tour sets out in relation to where you are staying, who is leading it, and meal and transportation arrangements. Compile a travel library with resources, books, and other information that will help you make the most of your journey.

> ### *Mary's Travel Gems*
>
> *One of the least expensive ways to turn a vacation into a learning adventure is to contact the local educational institution in the area you want to visit. Many colleges and universities can book you directly on historic tours, lectures, language intensives, work/study programs, and even offer inexpensive room and board.*
>
> *◇◇◇*

The more thorough your homework and preparation, the safer and more pleasant your trip will be.

✦ **Do your "hunch homework."** Any time you plan a specialty trip affiliated with an organization, you have an opportunity to find out firsthand what it is like by talking to past clients and getting a sense of the tour and tour operators. If an organization will not provide references, you are with the wrong outfit. Ask people who went on this trip if it was well organized. Did they get out of it what they expected? If there was a guide or director, did he or she speak English reasonably well? Was the leader competent and helpful? Do they have any advice for you? Would they recommend this organization? Talking to travelers who share your interests is the single best way to avoid problems.

✦ **Buy insurance.** Do I sound like a broken record yet on the subject of insurance? One out of every fifteen travelers has to fly home or be evacuated to a medical facility because of an accident or illness. When you are going on any kind of vacation, but especially when it is an adventure trip, you cannot be over insured. Getting sick or injured happens more frequently on adventure vacations than with any other type of travel.

✈ **Be a wise consumer before you sign up.** Find out what kind of insurance and waivers are required. Ask lots of questions about the tour guide, if there is one. Is the guide licensed and insured? Confirm the rates and find out exactly what is included in this price. If you will be on a group tour, ask about the demographics of the other people on the tour. You probably do not want to be the only forty-year-old in a group of college students, for example. Ask for a written agreement, and do not sign anything until you have read and understood the fine print. Never pay upfront or in cash without a written receipt.

> ### Adventure Guide Tip
>
> Ask your adventure guide what he does in his time off. If he doesn't do what he takes others to do, chances are good that someone else would be a better guide.

✈ **Listen to your inner voice.** If you are in Ireland learning the art of lace making, chances are you are having a mellow time. But if you are in the wilderness and your guide is pushing you to do something that feels dangerous, or group members are pressuring you to go faster or to deviate from the planned itinerary, it is imperative that you listen to your inner voice. I have learned from experience that if you feel uncomfortable, there is always a good reason for it. *That voice is your wiser self warning you.* Heed that inner guide and you will stay safe and healthy on any adventure.

> ### Let Uncle Sam Pick up the Tab
>
> Volunteer vacations and work-study trips are usually tax deductible as long as you can prove that the trip was not primarily recreational.

✈ **For volunteer vacations, bring a cooperative spirit.** Work vacations, sometimes called volunteer vacations, are becoming more popular as people combine service with travel. By agreeing to work part of the time, you cut down radically on the cost of your trip to an exotic locale, such as an underdeveloped community, an archaeological dig, or an unspoiled ecological region. These kinds of vacations can cost as little as $200! But do not forget that you are expected to work hard for this privilege, and you will probably not be staying in luxurious accommodations. Packing a good attitude and being mentally prepared to serve will help you get the most out of your working vacation.

10

Top Tips for Elderly and Disability Travel

I always say that each of us has special needs of one kind or another that we have to take into account when traveling far from home. You might be someone, for example, who suffers from severe headaches and mood drop if you do not eat exactly every four hours. Or perhaps you need to get a minimum of eight hours of sleep in order to function well and enjoy the day. We all learn to care for such needs when we are away from home and off our routine. This is especially true as we get older.

But if you have a limiting medical condition, physical disability, or are advanced in age, traveling may be more complicated and difficult. Fortunately, the travel industry is learning to accommodate the elderly and disabled in new and better ways.

Thanks to the Americans with Disabilities Act (ADA), buses, trains, and planes are now required to help you get from here to there. Each of these industries has created standard procedures for assisting travelers with special needs. Too, most hotels, tourist attractions, theatres, sports stadiums, resorts, and restaurants in the United States cannot turn you away and will make

Everything You Need to Know

Here is wonderful resource dedicated to everything there is to know about traveling with a disability. The Society for Accessible Travel & Hospitality (SATH) has a great website, www.sath.org, chock-full of advice, resources, up-to-date information, and travel ideas.

special arrangements for you whether you are in a wheelchair or have a disability such as a visual or hearing impairment. Even car rental companies offer specially equipped cars for the disabled. For this reason, the United States is a great place to travel if you have special needs.

A word about disability and elderly travel overseas: Even though other countries may not have laws like ADA that officially protect the rights of differently abled people, I have found foreigners to be particularly sensitive and accommodating to disabled and elderly travelers. Perhaps the kindness and respect I have witnessed arises from cultures that have deeply ingrained family values. From restaurateurs to taxi drivers, you will be pleasantly surprised at how foreigners go out of their way to serve your special needs. Be forewarned, however, that ramps and wheelchair-accessible bathrooms are not globally available, so it is important that you do your homework well before venturing abroad.

> ### What's Your Point?
>
> Here is a tip for everyone, especially those of us who are hearing impaired. When traveling abroad, get yourself a copy of the *International Travelers Point and Conversation Guide,* available from ArnMoor Publishing (407-855-5934). Divided into six main topics (services, shopping, sports and entertainment, transportation, accommodation, and food items), it allows you to point to what you need, no matter what the language or how softly it is spoken.

There are many books, websites, and organizations with useful information for elderly travelers, people with mobility issues, the sight or hearing impaired, diabetics, kidney patients, people requiring oxygen, and every other special or limiting condition imaginable. For help in getting special services on your trip, check out the resources I have included in the Appendix for all types of special needs.

About Wheelchairs and Scooters

Traveling with a wheelchair or scooter requires extra time, extra preparation, and certain responsibilities on your part. Since policies and regulations vary depending on the mode of transportation, the specific company, tour operator, and country, it is essential that you talk to a travel agent, do research on the internet, send for government literature, contact various travel companies, and visit your local library when planning to travel with a mobility impairment. Refer to the Appendix for extensive resources that can help.

In almost every country, transportation operators, whether bus, train, or air, will assist you if you are in a wheelchair or scooter, but some require that you reserve services and seating ahead of time. The amount of advance notice varies from company to company, so contact them directly. If you require a travel companion, that person often travels free of charge. In the United States and Canada, most cities have wheelchair-accessible public transportation, but in Europe the practice is less universal.

Amtrak train travel in the United States is also wheelchair accessible. Contact Amtrak directly to obtain a copy of their offerings and special facilities for wheelchair travelers.

If bus travel is your preference, Greyhound will assist wheelchair travelers, although they do not at press time have buses with chair lifts. If you contact the company, they will send you a copy of their travel policy brochure with details on handicapped travel.

Air travel with a wheelchair is trickier and requires that you be at the airport early. How much earlier than normal depends on the specific airline's preboarding requirements. You can usually use your own wheelchair or scooter up to the boarding point, where you will be transferred to a special aisle chair. Your wheelchair or scooter will be stowed and made available to you upon arrival. If you have an electric wheelchair, baggage handlers have to disconnect the leads from the battery terminal and cap them to avoid shorting. If your electric wheelchair or scooter has a wet-acid battery, as opposed to a dry cell or sealed-gel battery, baggage handlers will have to remove the wet-acid battery and place it in a special container. This requires that you be at the airport at least three hours before departure. Since each airline has a different policy for wheelchair travelers, call them in advance so you will be in compliance with their regulations.

Below are my top tips for travelers with special needs.

Service Dogs Not Welcome

Some island states have strict anti-rabies laws restricting the entrance of all animals, including service animals. Destinations with severe regulations and prolonged quarantines include Hawaii, Australia, New Zealand, and Ireland. Always contact the country's embassy before traveling abroad with your service dog.

✈ **Use a travel agent.** This I cannot emphasize enough. A travel agent knows your rights and responsibilities. She will make all the necessary phone calls and arrangements, and knows what questions to ask hotels and tour groups and which accommodations to request. She can find you a hotel, for example, that has closed captioned television and special alarms and phones for the hearing impaired. She has clout in securing a room that is close to the elevator, or in finding a transportation company that offers a wheelchair lift. If you travel with a service animal, she will know what type of documentation your dog requires. She will also find you the right travel insurance for your specific set of circumstances. She will no doubt think of things you forgot, such as booking you a seat near the restroom and on the aisle for easy mobility. Ask your travel agent to verbally walk you through the security procedures at airports and customs so you will be prepared for issues that could come up regarding prosthetic devices, canes and walkers, syringes and other medical equipment, and X-ray damage. In the event

Pacemaker Pat-Down

If you have a pacemaker, notify security screeners beforehand and ask for a pat-down inspection rather than walking through the metal detector or being hand-wanded. A Pacemaker ID card from your doctor or hospital is helpful in these situations.

that you encounter discriminative practices or uncooperative people on your trip, your trusty travel agent will be your staunchest advocate.

✈ **Notify transportation companies and personnel well in advance.** Most travel professionals will jump through hoops to help you as long as you give them proper notice. If traveling by air, notify the airlines, under the code SSR (Special Service Request) or OSI (Other Service Information), of your status and the special services you will need. You need to do this at least forty-eight hours before flight time. Do not forget that if you are changing planes, trains, or buses, you will need the assistance of ground personnel at those transfer points to help you make connections.

✈ **Homework is essential.** Every medical condition and physical limitation comes with its own problems vis-à-vis traveling. For example, if you are flying and require an oxygen tank, you will need a doctor's prescription, and will have to pay to use the airline's equipment. You will not be permitted to use your own, due to safety requirements. Rather than getting cross or feeling victimized, do your homework so you will be prepared for, not surprised by, unpleasantries and inconveniences.

> **Baby Your Mature Skin**
>
> The older your skin, the more susceptible it is to sunburn. Wear lots of sunscreen and keep skin moisturized, as it gets thinner with age and can crack more easily.

✈ **Meet with your doctor before you go.** It sounds like a no-brainer, but many of us have gotten so used to our disabilities and physical limitations that we do not think of the potential perils inherent in traveling. It is important to talk to your doctor ahead of time, not only to obtain extra supplies of medication and to get copies of your prescriptions, but also to discuss your trip and special needs in detail. If you are a diabetic, for example, traveling abroad through different time zones can wreak havoc on your medication schedule. Some diabetics also experience adverse reactions to vaccinations, diarrhea or nausea medicines, and exotic foods and drinks. Go prepared with a list of questions, and do listen to your doctor's advice.

✈ **Safeguard your medications.** Carry several days' supply of medicine in your carry-on luggage. Have your doctor give you a synopsis of your condition and copies of prescriptions in case you would have a medical emergency away from home. Keep a list of medications you are carrying with your other important documents, on your person, and be ready to show them to customs if you are crossing international borders.

> ### Worldwide Dialysis
>
> You do not have to give up travel if you require kidney dialysis. There are dialysis centers all around the world that will serve you if you notify them in advance, and even special cruises that offer dialysis onboard. For more information, contact the National Kidney Foundation, 800-622-9010.

✈ **Protect your wheelchair or scooter.** As a precaution against loss or damage, remove all detachable parts before your wheelchair or scooter is stored, and label it with your name and an identifying address (but not your own home address) and destination airport. Make sure your travel insurance covers loss or damage of your wheelchair or scooter.

✈ **Choose your destination with care.** The best way to have a successful trip is to be realistic about your physical limitations. Choose a hotel that is accessible even if you are not in a wheelchair. Find one in a suitable environment with lots of outdoor seating, pools, shady spots, and facilities nearby. Select a destination that offers tours and excursions for people with limited mobility. Big, polluted cities and high-altitude locations are not healthy places for you if you are elderly or have respiratory problems.

✈ **Get into a mellow mindset**. You will have a great time if you just relax and accept the fact that you may need to preboard, wait for assistance, and depend on others for help, often unskilled and inexperienced people who are nevertheless well meaning. My advice is to bring along a good book or audiobook and get into the groove of a more leisurely pace. Also, do not overprogram your trip. Allow plenty of time to relax and rest. Do not try to fill up every minute.

✈ **Take extra care in the air.** Flying is particularly hard on the elderly. Lack of exercise in airports and in cramped planes can cause complications if your circulation is bad to begin with. Get up and move around at least once every half hour, if possible, and do leg, ankle, and feet stretches. Angina and breathlessness are also exacerbated by flying. If notified in advance, the airline will provide oxygen for you.

> ### Mary's Travel Gems
>
> *How many times have you seen elderly people pulled aside by airport security and asked to take off their shoes? It may be because they are wearing comfortable Rockport brand shoes. Rockports have metal inside their sole that sets off the security alarm!* ✦✦✦

✈ **Never stand when you can sit.** And never sit when you can lie down! Why would you go on a trip in order to push yourself to the brink of exhaustion? Take every opportunity to relax to the max and I guarantee you will have a better experience.

✈ **Scope out the bathroom at each stop.** Whether you are shopping, eating out, or sightseeing, take a moment to locate the nearest bathroom, because when you need to go, you do not want to be looking around desperately to find one. Scarcity of toilets is one of the great inconveniences of traveling. Never pass up the chance to use toilet facilities, since you do not know when or where the next one will turn up. Always carry with you a pack of tissue to use for toilet paper or to cover the toilet seat.

> ## The Kindness of Strangers
>
> I led a 10-day Mediterranean tour with 55 people, including a woman whose knees were fused together since birth. While in Granada, Spain, we visited an Arabian villa perched atop a hill with hundreds of steps. All the guys took turns carrying her and her wheelchair so she wouldn't miss out. It made the whole trip a joy for all of us.

✈ **Patronize the good guys.** We can all make this world a better place by supporting the companies that serve people with special needs. For example, if your eyesight is poor but you can still get around by yourself, seek out a "slow walker" tour, designed for people who wish to see the sights but need to stop more frequently, for longer periods of time, in order to take it all in. If you have a hearing impairment, find a hotel that has closed-captioned television services and offers light alarms. If you have difficulty walking, seek out a cruise line that serves wheelchair travelers. In other words, make your world fit you, not the other way around. The more we patronize the good guys, the better off we will all be.

11

Top Tips for Traveling with Pets

Traveling with pets can be tricky, although it is not impossible. First of all, you should know that taking your dog or cat on a trip limits your mode of travel. Trains, for instance, are out. Amtrak does not permit pets of any kind, except for seeing-eye dogs. Local and commuter trains have their own policies. Greyhound and other bus companies also prohibit live animals except for seeing-eye dogs. If traveling by ship, there is only one cruise line I am aware of that allows pets: the *QE2* luxury liner. The *QE2* provides special lodging and free meals for your dog. The ship has air-conditioned kennels and an open-air exercise area where you can walk your dog. But there are some restrictions. You can only take pets on transatlantic crossings, for example, and you can only visit your pet during preset visiting hours. Also, the fee is quite hefty: $500 at this writing. To find smaller boating and charter companies that welcome pets, see the Appendix.

www.companionair.com

Companion air is a new airline dedicated to providing high-quality, specialized transportation to pet lovers and their pets. The planes feature pet cabins where you can visit your pet during the flight. If you love traveling with your pet, support this airline!

That leaves the two most common options: driving or flying. Driving is the easiest, most convenient, and cheapest mode. It is also the most comfortable for your pet, because you can regulate air temperature, offer plenty of exercise stops, and monitor your pet's emotional state.

Flying is expensive and gives you less control. Every airline has different regulations regarding pets, so call and get the details *before* you make reservations. Find out if they take your kind of pet, and find out what they charge. At this writing, the average fee was $50 per pet. Ask about age and size restrictions. And definitely ask about their first-come, first-served policy, since some airlines only allow one pet in first class, one in business class, and so on. Also, be aware that most airlines reserve the right to refuse travel if there are too many pets onboard.

I adore my cats, and that is why I leave them at home with a sitter where they can be safe, healthy, and secure in familiar surroundings. The only time I have traveled with all of them together is when I was relocating from one state to another. Think of your pets the way you might think of an elderly parent. Unless they really need to take the trip, they would be more comfortable staying home.

> **Before Taking Fido Along— Answer the Following Questions Honestly:**
>
> • Would he be better off at home?
>
> • Will he be able to do most of our activities with us?
>
> • Will he be spending most of his time in the kennel?

Travel is more stressful for animals than for people because they have no way of knowing what is happening. A vacation may mean time to relax for you, but for your pet, it means unfamiliar sights, sounds, and smells, which can be disconcerting.

If you decide to fly with a small pet, I recommend the Sherpa Bag, a soft pet carrier available from most pet stores. Designed by a flight attendant, it fits under an airline seat, has see-through mesh "windows," a shoulder strap that doubles as a leash, and many other pet- and owner-friendly features.

There are many helpful information sources on the internet. Some will tell you the specific pet-related policies of each airline, others offer travel tips for just about any type of pet—rodents, fish, and reptiles included.

There are also good sites that list pet-friendly campgrounds, beaches, hotels, and resorts.

A lot can go wrong when you travel with pets. Here are my top tips for preventing most common problems.

✈ **Before long drives with your pet, make a pet itinerary.** There are lots of hotels and motels that take pets, but more that do not. Never assume that they will allow your pet to stay, and do not try to sneak your pet into your room. Instead, spend some time on the internet or at your local bookstore before your trip finding out the names and locations of pet-friendly places along your route.

✈ **Know the local regulations beforehand.** In this country, we rarely think about getting stopped and questioned by authorities. But every state has regulations regarding animals and it is a good idea to find out what they are before you take your pet on a trip. If your dog got loose in a campground or rest stop, for instance, you could be ticketed if his rabies shots were not up-to-date. Some states require an entry permit issued by the destination state's regulatory agency, regardless of your mode of transportation. Some states even have border inspections.

> ### Bring Your Fish to Alaska
>
> If you are moving to Alaska and want to bring Goldie the Goldfish with you, you're in luck. Alaska Airlines is one of the few air carriers that's "fish friendly."

✈ **Get your pet used to kennel and car.** If the only times your pet is kenneled or takes a car trip is when you board him or take him to the vet, he will have negative associations with being transported. Before taking him on a trip, make a few practice runs in the car. Give him lots of praise, love, and rewards after each trip. Put treats in his kennel and keep the kennel in your house or yard for a couple weeks before the trip. Doing this will enable your pet to feel safer and be calmer as you set out on your travels together.

✈ **Keep your pet leashed, harnessed, or kenneled inside the car.** You know your pet best. Some pets do better kenneled inside the car than others. Kenneled or not, however, it is a good idea to keep a leash or harness on your pet. You might even want to attach his leash or harness to a seat belt. If your animal were to jump out of the car and get loose in heavy traffic, it would be disastrous. Expect the unexpected, as I always say, and then take the necessary precautions.

✈ **Make his comfort level a priority.** Make sure the kennel is the proper size. Your pet should be able to stand up with head erect, sit, lie down, and turn around comfortably. The kennel door should have a secure lock, but never one with a key or combination lock, in case it has to be opened in an emergency. Put a favorite blanket, toy, or piece of your clothing in the kennel with him before you set out. New research suggests that our pheromones trigger a calming response in dogs.

Pet Travel Items to Pack

Here is a short list of items you will need when traveling with your pet:

- Grooming tools
- Favorite blanket and toys
- Treats
- Room deodorizer
- Stain remover
- Pooper scooper and baggies
- Extra leash and collars
- Vitamins and medications
- ID and vaccine tags
- Medical records
- Pet food and jug of water from home (own water helps prevent stomach upset)
- Food and water dishes
- Can opener

✈ **Feed, water, and exercise before flying.** A general rule of thumb is to feed your pet no less than five or six hours before the flight, and to give him a drink of water no less than two hours before. Give him the chance to walk outside just prior to departure. If there are long and unexpected delays, you will have done your best to ensure his health and comfort.

Some airlines require you to place food and water in the kennel or in attached containers for emergencies.

✈ **Do not sedate your pet on a flight.** High altitudes and sedatives can be a dangerous combination. If your pet is so high-strung that you or your vet thinks he requires sedation, I recommend that you reconsider your decision to fly. Driving would be a better and safer option for your pet.

✈ **Identification and documentation are essential.** Protect your pet in case the two of you are separated. He should wear an identification tag with his name and your number on it. The kennel, too, should be clearly marked with his name and your number. Keep on your person your pet's papers along with your own medical documents. His papers should include his name, home address, phone number, and medical records.

✈ **Arrange to have your pet in the cabin, not cargo, if possible.** If you have a large pet, you are out of luck. But if your travel companion is a cat or small dog, contact the airline well ahead of time and find out how to transport him onboard with you. There are only a certain number of animals allowed in the cabin, determined on a first-come, first-served basis. I would never place my pet in cargo if I did not have to. The cargo area is cold and there is no way to control the temperature down there. I have also read awful stories about animals escaping from their kennels in the cargo area due to careless baggage handlers. If these loose animals jump onto the tarmac after landing, their fate is not a pretty one. Make sure you have the pet's leash with you in your carry-on, not packed away.

✈ **Help him adjust to new surroundings upon arrival.** Even though you are there, your pet will still go through an adjustment period upon arrival. New water, new surroundings, new sounds and smells are all disconcerting, so it is a good idea to keep your pet leashed or harnessed at all times. Cats in particular should be kept indoors, as their instinct is to try to find their way back "home."

✈ **Purchase pet insurance.** Pet insurance is not expensive, and I recommend it for your pet for the same reasons that I recommend it for people. See the Appendix for sources.

12
Top Tips for Healthy Travel

Have you ever gotten back from a trip and found that you needed a vacation from your vacation? Traveling wears you out, physically and emotionally. It gets you out of your normal eating, exercising, and sleeping routine. And it exposes you to new worlds—of germs, bacteria, and viruses. If you feel drained and sick after traveling, it is no wonder.

Fortunately, you can do something about it. From traveling all over the world for many years now, I have learned some great ways to stay energized and illness-free. Typing in a phrase such as *travel health* on a good internet search engine will yield dozens of great sites that feature travel-related health products, health advisories, and articles on maintaining fitness away from home. Be sure to check out my recommendations in the Appendix for excellent books, websites, and organizations devoted to keeping you healthy away from home.

Here are my top tips for healthy travel.

✈ **Talk to your doc.** Before you head off on an international journey, pay a visit to your family physician. My doctor, for example, advised me to get a flu shot, even though it was summertime here. I was getting ready to travel halfway across the world, where flu season was already in full swing. This bit of wisdom was something that never would have occurred to me. He also wrote me a prescription for a broad-spectrum antibiotic that

Know Your Heart

Cardiovascular disease is the leading cause of death among international travelers, accounting for 50% of the deaths among American travelers 60 years and older. Medical experts attribute this to prolonged sitting, oxygen deprivation aboard aircraft and at higher altitudes, hot and cold environments, and sudden spurts of physical activity, such as carrying heavy luggage.

would clear up just about any bacterial infection, just in case. As I always remind others, it never hurts to get a physical before a long trip. When was the last time you had one?

✦ **Be a germ detective.** At home, I am quite relaxed about germs. But when I travel, I turn into a hyper-alert antigerm spy. I carry my own pillowcase to lean my head against instead of the airplane-seat headrest. I only drink beverages that come out of sealed containers, preferably water. I wash my hands many times a day, and carry water-free hand cleaner or moist towelettes everywhere I go. I take the bedspread off my hotel bed first thing and store it in the corner. I never eat street food, and if I buy fresh fruit, I wash it thoroughly with bottled water before I eat it. It only takes one microscopic bug hitchhiking on a flight-attendant's hand, on a public telephone, or on a piece of fruit to ruin your trip.

The 45-Minute Waker-Upper

NASA research has found that a 45-minute nap greatly improves alertness. Longer naps leave you feeling groggy.

✦ **Do not over-schedule.** If you try to cram back-to-back meetings into a business trip, you will be in for an unpleasant surprise. Your alertness will suffer, your energy will lag, and chances are you will not feel great upon returning home. Peak performance and productivity on business trips result from high-quality sleep and rest, physical activity, and light, healthy meals. I always remind my business associates that an hour off here or there is not going to make or break a deal. Give that hour to yourself—for a meditative stroll or for a nap—and watch what happens when you go into your next meeting fresh. On a recent trip to Geneva, Switzerland, in the second day of conferences, I was surprised at how fuzzy-minded I was. Was I experiencing a heavy dose of jet lag? Was it something I ate? It turns out that my body had not acclimated to the 3,000-foot elevation.

✈ **Fit in three ten-minute activities each day.** Most experts agree that thirty minutes of exercise a day can make an enormous difference in the way you feel and function. Going to the hotel workout room is the obvious way to accomplish this modest fitness goal. But when my business days are hectic and I cannot spare a half-hour, I try to figure out three times during the day when I can squeeze in a ten-minute activity. These are easy things I can do that will get my heart rate up, sharpen my mind, and give me energy. Here are some of my favorites: stretching and doing floor exercises while watching the morning headlines on TV; walking up and down four flights of hotel stairs three times; parking two blocks away from my meeting; taking stairs instead of elevators; and walking briskly through a mall or convention area.

✈ **Avoid too much salt, alcohol, and sugar.** Any member of this trio can wreak havoc on your energy and vitality on the road. Too much salt makes you lethargic, particularly if you have high blood pressure. Alcohol tends to have a stronger effect on travelers, especially when

Swim At Your Own Risk

When in exotic locales, don't just swim or wade anywhere, no matter how sparkling the water looks. Watering holes in South Africa, sub-Saharan Africa, Lake Malawi, and the Nile River Valley in Egypt, for instance, carry a parasitic disease known as bilharzia, which you can get just by dipping your toes.

How to "Run" a Meeting

Joanne V. Lichten, author of *How to Stay Healthy and Fit on the Road,* recommends inviting a business associate to a working-out lunch, where you talk business while walking or using exercise equipment.

paired with the high-altitude of flying. Dry hotel room air plus too much alcohol can dehydrate you and give you a whopping headache in the morning. Sugar completes the mischievous trio. Experts say eating too much refined sugar found in doughnuts, cookies, breads, buns, and pastries whacks out your blood sugar, or glucose, production and will make you moody, irritable, and fatigued.

✈ **Book a hotel room that has a refrigerator.** The biggest adjustment problem I have every time I travel is being away from the food I love and my own eating routine. For many travelers, eating out three meals a day translates into extra pounds, sluggishness, and feeling "off" from eating food to which you are unaccustomed. Having a refrigerator in my hotel room solves several problems at once. I store purchased fruit, juice, carrots, and cheese in there to have for healthy snacks or to eat instead of a huge lunch. And I have leftovers from large meals wrapped to go, which I can then eat for lunch or breakfast the next day. (Have you ever had pasta primavera for breakfast? Yummy!) Having a refrigerator helps me save money and puts me in control of how much I eat out. I also find that eating a quiet lunch alone in my room, when I am able to, restores my sanity and helps me collect my thoughts.

✈ **Drink only bottled water, and drink lots of it.** There is a quiet controversy bubbling up on the safety of drinking water on airplanes. The FDA is starting a program to test airline water, which we may be hearing more about in the coming months. Do what I do: Purchase one or two six-packs of bottled water before you leave so you can have a bottle with you at all times: in the car, on the train or plane, in your day pack while sight-seeing, and in your hotel room. Experts say drinking lots of water is one of the best ways to combat jet lag, flush out toxins, keep your body hydrated for maximum function, and help you stay healthy. I also find that the coffee and tea I make in hotel room coffeemakers tastes better when made with bottled water.

✈ **Take care of your emotional health, too.** Grownup homesickness is real. As I mentioned earlier, my husband used to tell me he could set a clock by my first forlorn phone call, which always happens exactly three days into every trip. Bring along one or two favorite comfort items from home, such as a photo, stuffed animal, hot-water bottle, lap blanket, or pillow. Take care of unfinished business before you leave so you do not obsess about it while you are away. Take extra measures to fight stress and induce calm, such as hot baths, naps, more downtime than usual, meditation, or reading. Treat yourself to something indulgent on your trip, such as a pedicure, a piece of jewelry, or breakfast in bed.

> ### Travel with Electrolytes
>
> Diarrhea, a.k.a. "traveler's revenge," is a common cause of dehydration, sometime serious. I always pack in my first aid kit a few electrolyte packets. Dissolved in water, they restore important minerals. Check travel product catalogs or health food stores.

> ### Mary's Travel Gems
>
> *Smart companies are booking more of their business conferences and annual brainstorming retreats aboard cruise ships. Conducting business at sea is the ultimate way to combine high-powered meetings with fresh air, fitness, healthy food, and relaxing activities.* ❖❖❖

Appendix

*A Note to Readers: Doing your homework is the single best way you can prepare for and hopefully avoid disasters, mishaps, illness, injury, victimization, and other unpleasant and unexpected travel circumstances. I strongly urge you to use the resources in the pages that follow. I like to bookmark my favorite websites and return to them frequently for updated news and articles. The world's travel climate is ever changing, so arm yourself with the most up-to-date information you can find. Be sure to visit my website, **www.travelresourcecenter.com,** where I will be posting new travel tips on an ongoing basis. Once you get the hang of doing travel-related research, you will no doubt find favorite websites and resources of your own. Happy exploring!*

General Travel Information

Automobile Club of America (AAA)
www.aaa.com

This is not your father's triple-A. This wonderful organization is now a full-service travel agency. By joining, you get discounts on car rentals, hotels, airline tickets, cruises, vacation planning services, lodging, motor/RV touring, theme parks, and national park passes. Membership privileges include RV and road trip planning (TripTiks) and emergency roadside service, as well as international driving permits, travelers checks, and foreign currency transactions. AAA is a truly international organization with offices and service locations worldwide. The wonderful website has great information about luggage, locks, books, maps, international road signs, gas prices, local weather and road conditions, passport requirements, and much more. This is a great site to visit for valuable information and tips about any kind of trip you might be thinking of taking.

Better Business Bureau (BBB)
www.bbb.org
Phone: (703) 276-0200 • Fax: (703) 525-8277

Every consumer should bookmark this website, and that includes travel consumers. Here is where you will find helpful articles on topics including business travel costs, lost luggage, spring break, and how to protect yourself against travel scams. Also, learn how to file a complaint against an unscrupulous provider of a travel service, such as a hotel, travel agent, car rental company, or tour company.

Currency Conversion
www.xe.com/ucc

Here is a nifty idea: a universal currency converter that allows you to perform interactive foreign exchange-rate calculations right on the internet, using live, up-to-the-minute currency rates. To find out how far your dollar will go, just punch in a dollar amount, click on the country you will be visiting, and *voila,* you get an instant conversion. How cool is that for planning your trip abroad?

Federal Citizen Information Center
www.pueblo.gsa.gov

This all-American website offers free or nearly free government-issued booklets on a variety of topics, including your rights as an airline passenger, personal security, tips for women traveling alone, travel tips for students, travelers' health on cruise ships and planes, and traveling with a disability. There are also useful links to related sites on every topic imaginable. This is a goldmine of information for anyone starting to plan a trip who needs to know about documentation, regulations, your rights and options as a smart consumer, and more.

Maps.com
www.maps.com

Want a map of anywhere in the world? Maps.com has it—for free! This website attracts a reported 1.7 million users per month and is your one-stop site for maps of all sorts, from wall to digital. You can also use the site to get driving directions or to find an address. Pick a place, no matter how remote, and maps.com will find it. If you zoom in for more detail, you can even get the names of tiny rural roads. This is an unbeatable resource for driving trips and adventure travel to off-the-beaten-track places.

NewsDirectory
www.NewsDirectory.com/travel/

This stripped-down information site, or virtual library, is quite useful if you will be traveling within the United States. Simply click on a destination state and you will be whisked to a page that is nothing but hot links to visitors bureaus organized by city, as well as area airports, newspapers, colleges, city government offices, hotels, rental cars, and more. This free directory can help you get to where you want to go, or find sites you did not know about. NewsDirectory provides a simple and fast way to access all the news and information that you can handle about places you want to visit.

PassengerRights.com
www.PassengerRights.com

A website designed to help protect and assist the travel consumer. This group of do-gooders has done all the necessary research for every type of complaint travelers may have, and has compiled hundreds of email addresses so that your complaint will be forwarded to the appropriate parties. This website also provides guidance on how to write and file complaints, and posts dozens of horror stories that are interesting to read and that make you feel either lucky or not so alone.

QuickAid.com Airport Directory
www.quickaid.com

Want to find out more about an airport? This is the place to do it online. Click on an airport anywhere in the world to get phone numbers for the airport and to find out about on-premise and area hotels, rental cars, airport parking and ground transportation information, terminal maps, area maps, and even airport statistics.

Rudy Maxa, The Savvy Traveler
www.rudymaxa.com
(800) 387-8025

Rudy Maxa, of National Public Radio's popular travel show, *The Savvy Traveler,* offers a fantastic website that is informative and fun to read. Read well-written, well-researched articles and essays about saving money, saving time, and staying healthy and safe. He lists deals, best-kept secret destinations, and has interesting insights to share on every topic related to travel. I always learn something when I browse this website. If you are a travel buff, this is a great site to bookmark.

Tourism Offices Worldwide Directory
www.towd.com

As its name suggest, this site lists 1,445 official government tourist offices, convention and visitors bureaus, chambers of commerce, and similar agencies worldwide that provide free, accurate, and unbiased travel information to the public. It does not list travel agents, tour operators, or hotels. Use the drop-down boxes at the top to search by country or state

Travel Time—Trains & Subways
www.vais.net/~traveltime/index.html
Phone: (800) 856-2781 • Fax: (703) 866-1317

Travel Time is a Virginia-based travel agency with good online resources for travelers, but I cite it here especially for train enthusiasts. The above address takes you right to the Trains page, which has detailed information about rail and subway travel everywhere in the world, with a special section for student travelers.

Travel Health Resources

Centers for Disease Control and Prevention (CDC)
www.cdc.gov
(800) 232-2522, National Immunization Hotline
(800) 311-3435, Travelers Health Information

An excellent online resource with updated health information for travelers and health-related articles about such issues as terrorism and the latest smallpox news. Clicking on "Travelers' Health" from the menu takes you to a page where you can access health information by region and read about recent outbreaks, diseases, and vaccinations. The site also has good information about traveling with children, special needs, and specific cruise ship health reports. Many of CDC's excellent publications can be viewed and downloaded for free from your own computer.

International Association for Medical Assistance for Travelers (IAMAT)
www.iamat.org
(716) 754-4883

Worldwide membership in this nonprofit organization is free, but they take donations. The website features a directory of English-speaking medical providers, world climate charts, malaria risk charts, and other travel medicine information based on World Health Organization information and expert sources. You will also find a world immunization chart: required and recommended immunizations, routine and specific immunizations for selected groups of travelers and persons on working assignments, and the geographical distribution of hepatitis B, Japanese encephalitis, plague, rabies, tick-borne encephalitis, and yellow fever. You can subscribe to the e-newsletter for free.

International Society of Travel Medicine (ISTM)
www.istm.org
Phone: (770) 736-7060 • Fax: (770) 736-6732

This is the website of the largest organization of professionals dedicated to the specialty of travel medicine. Check out the awesome ISTM Clinic Directory, with more than 500 travel medicine clinics representing more than 40 countries included. I highly recommend that you print out the names and contact information for all clinics in the countries to which you will be traveling. This is a valuable resource for travelers.

World Health Organization (WHO)
www.who.int
Phone: (202) 974-3000 • Fax: (202) 974-3663

This United Nations agency has a good website with recent and breaking health news from around the world. International travelers can access information by country or by disease, and view traveler's checklists and questionnaires pertaining to vaccinations, illness prevention, local diseases, accidents, and other topics. This is a good source to find out more about traveler's insurance, special needs travel, travel medications, environmental health risks, injuries and violence, and blood transfusions. WHO also publishes a number of traveler's health resources that you can purchase online.

Travel Safety, Security, and Documentation Resources

Federal Aviation Administration (FAA)
www.faa.gov
Phone: (202) 267-9165 • Fax: (202) 493-5032

For the traveler, this government agency website has a few noteworthy items, most of them security-related. Here is where you can get security tips and find out about airline on-time statistics and safety data. The Air Traffic Control System Command Center has a national map of airports at the website. By clicking on any airport, you can find out if flights are arriving and departing on time, and if not, why not. This information is updated about every fifteen minutes.

Transportation Security Administration (TSA)
www.tsa.gov

This website offers traveler tips based on post-9/11 security regulations, such as warnings about locking your luggage and lists of newly prohibited carry-on items. There is also information here about what to wear and what to pack that will help you get through security more quickly.

U.S. State Department
www.travel.state.gov

Before you travel abroad, definitely check out this government website. Think of this website as the "where to go if . . . and what to do if . . ." website for Americans in other countries. You can print out information sheets with consular information for every country you are visiting. If anything were to happen to you abroad, you would have the most reliable email, phone number, and physical address of the officials whose job it is to assist you. You can also print out lists of hospitals and doctors in your destination country. Here is where you will find every kind of emergency contact, from where to go for emergency financial assistance and whom to contact if you are arrested, to where to seek safety in the event of an attack. The website has all kinds of other traveler information regarding passports, visas, overseas security, travel warnings, and much more. An hour looking over this website and printing out emergency numbers could be the hour that saved your life.

Passport Services

National Passport Information Center
travel.state.gov/passport_services.html
(900) 225-5674

Before you go to an expeditor, read through the tips and answers at the State Department,s National Passport Information Center website. The State Department may be able to get you your passport in time. This site also has information about what to do in the case of an emergency trip necessitated by the death of a loved one. If you have ever stood in line for a visa or passport, you know how time-consuming it can be. If you wish to skip the experience, you can easily find an expeditor in your area by typing *visa and passport expeditors* into Google. There are many such companies scattered throughout the United States.

Traveler's Medical Insurance

There are dozens of companies that sell medical insurance to travelers. To find a good one, (1) ask your travel agent whom she recommends; (2) type *travelers medical insurance* into Google or another good search engine on the web; (3) check out the companies listed on the U.S. State Department website, at **travel.state.gov/medical.html;** or (4) ask a friend who travels frequently. Business travelers are good bets, as their businesses often require them to buy traveler's insurance. Here are some other helpful resources:

Insure My Trip
www.insuremytrip.com
(800) 487-4722

This is a free travel insurance comparison site that offers thirty different plans from eleven different companies. A great way to see what is out there and to comparison shop. Be certain to examine the fine print for each policy.

Medjet Assistance
www.medjetassistance.com
Phone: (800) 963-3538 • Fax: (800) 863-3538

This is not travel insurance, but if you are ever hospitalized more than 150 miles from home, Medjet will fly you to the hospital of your choice at no charge in a medically equipped and staffed aircraft. Prepaid annual memberships for individuals up to 75 years of age are $195 and it covers everything. Families are $295. Groups and corporate rates are also available. If you travel a lot, have medical worries, or have very special doctors whom you trust, this could be a good way to go.

Fear of Flying

There are many programs for you if you are afraid of flying. Among major U.S. airlines, Northwest operates Wings, a series of weekend seminars in Minneapolis and Detroit. The program claims a 90 percent success rate. Type *fear of flying* into Google and see what comes up. Here are some other resources.

The Anxiety Bookstore
www.anxietybookstore.com
(214) 672-0564

Over 200 titles on anxiety disorders, including fear of flying.

Fear of Flying Clinic

www.fofc.com

(650) 341-1595

Based at San Francisco International Airport.

Fearless Flying

fearlessflying.com

Based on the Northwest Airlines WINGS seminars, this program uses audio- and videotapes, handbook, breathing tube, and relaxation techniques.

SOAR

www.fearofflying.com

(800) 332-7359

A program with study materials, audiotapes, and a manual, with one-on-one phone or in-person counseling with a licensed therapist.

Recreational Vehicle (RV) Information

Recreational Vehicle Rental Association (RVRA)

www.rvra.org

This is a national association of dealers who rent recreational vehicles. Visit the website to locate a rental dealer in your area and to get information about RV rentals and travel.

Trailer Life Magazine/Motorhome Magazine

www.trailerlife.com

At the website, you can sign up to receive their free quarterly newsletter with all kinds of news for the avid RVer. If you get into it, you might consider subscribing to one or both print magazines.

Travel Agent Information

American Society of Travel Agents (ASTA)

www.astanet.com

Phone: (800) 440-ASTA • Fax: (703) 684-8319

This is the website for the largest professional association for travel agents. Although a lot of the information on the site targets industry insiders, there is good information here for consumers as well. You can fill out a form to find a member travel agent, or you can request a trip and have an agent who specializes in that destination contact you. You can also read articles about passenger rights, travel agents, hot destinations, tips for passengers who have booked with bankrupt airlines, health and safety tips for travelers, and travel alerts.

International Cellular Service

I have had the greatest experience with renting cell phones when I traveled abroad. There are lots of great companies that will rent you a phone, preprogram your countries, and even provide you with emergency numbers. I was very happy with **World Cell (www.worldcell.com),** but there are many other such companies. I recommend typing *international cellular service* or *international cell phone rental* into Google and see what comes up.

Travel Gadgets, Essentials, and Attire

AJ Prindle & Co.

www.ajprindle.com

This online mail-order company offers unique products in a fun, easy-to-understand lifestyle format geared for road travelers. It has all kinds of safety and security products, great stuff for pet travel, and lots of other goodies to help you adapt your vehicle to fit the way you work, live, and play.

Christine Columbus

www.christinecolumbus.com
Phone: (800) 280-4775 • Fax: (800) 803-5383

Here you will find unique women's travel gear in a catalog containing lots of travel wear, luggage, books, gadgets, and essential travel products for safety, comfort, and convenience.

Magellan's

www.magellans.com
Phone: (800) 962-4943 • Fax: (800) 962-4940

A good online vendor of travel supplies, including appliances, security items, health and hygiene aids, and nifty packing and luggage accessories.

TravelProducts.com

www.travelproducts.com
Phone: (800) 917-4616 • Fax: (509) 753-3708

TravelProducts.com has been selling items for travelers online since the start of e-commerce in 1995. This company provides a huge selection of travel-sized essentials and conveniences to improve travel and the mobile lifestyle.

Travelsmith

www.travelsmith.com
Phone: (800) 950-1600 • Fax: (800) 950-1656

This company issues a wonderful colorful catalog with top-of-the-line travel clothes for men and women, from casual to professional attire, as well as luggage, footwear, gifts, and hats.

Traveling Solo

Connecting Solo Travel Network

www.cstn.org
Phone: (604) 886-9099 • Fax: (626) 608-2139

Connecting is a not-for-profit, international organization of individuals interested in sharing going-solo tips, news about single-friendly trips, and in promoting hospitality and goodwill among solo travelers everywhere. If you are serious about traveling solo, get a one-year membership. It costs $35 Canadian, which is about $24 American, and entitles you to six newsletters, a single-friendly travel directory, unlimited travel companion advertising, advice and hospitality exchanges, and member discounts.

Traveling with Children

Family Adventure Travel

www.familyadventuretravel.com

Here is a great website brought to you by the folks who publish *Family Adventure Magazine,* a magazine devoted to adventure traveling with kids throughout the world. At the website you can search for family-friendly tour companies by activity, such as horseback riding, skiing, or bicycling, and by region of the world. This is a great "ideas" website for planning your next summer vacation with the kids, or for creating educational/adventure trips for youth groups or summer campers. You can also read all kinds of articles about traveling with children, or click on "Howie's Bookshelf," a list of family adventure travel books with mini-reviews. If you like what you see here and travel frequently with children, an annual subscription to the magazine is only $10/year. Subscription details are on the website.

Family Fun
www.family.go.com

Brought to you by the publishers of *Family Fun* magazine, this helpful website has a whole section devoted to traveling with kids. It includes articles, guides to family-friendly vacation spots, activities you can do with kids while traveling, and great travel checklists that you can print out and tuck in your pocket, for everything from pet travel needs and car trip essentials to stocking your first-aid kit and beach trip packing.

Business Travel

Joe Sent Me, the Homepage for Business Travelers
www.joesentme.com

For the business traveler, travel journalist Joe Brancatelli has put together a great weekly e-newletter with hints, tips, commentary, and steals and deals aplenty. The newsletter is free, but donations are appreciated. Joe is an opinionated, colorful writer who understands the needs of business travelers like few others. I love reading Joe's pieces, and I have picked up many great tips from him.

Lifestyle and Specialty Travel

Specialty Travel Index
www.spectrav.com
Phone: (800) 442-4922 • Fax: (415) 459-4974

From the publishers of the eponymous print magazine, here is a great website with links to and information on over 500 tour operators worldwide offering trips for the adventure and special interest traveler. At the website you can search by destination, activity, or tour operation. Also, read fun travel stories from writers each month recounting their excellent adventures. This is a good "idea" site if you want to do something new, but lack the imagination to conceive it.

Elderly and Disability Travel

Access-Able Travel Source
www.access-able.com
Phone: (303) 232-2979 • Fax: (303) 239-8486

This is one of the best and most comprehensive sites for disabled travelers that I have come across. The website has free information on everything you need to know about travel with disabilities, mature travel, disability magazines, access guides, wheelchair travel, scooter rental, accessible transportation, and more. You can find out about world destinations—details about accommodations, attractions, transportation, equipment rental and repairs, and even adventures; travel professionals—travel agents and tour operators who specialize in disability travel; and cruise ships. A searchable database that is user-friendly makes it easy to find what you need to know. This is an excellent source of books, magazines, newsletters, and organizations that have your needs in mind, as well.

The Accessible Guide for Specialized Ground Transportation
www.accessibletransport.com
Phone: (866) 392-2876, PIN 5770

This is a comprehensive and up-to-date resource that provides a quick and easy way to locate specialized ground transportation to airports, hotels, restaurants, business meetings, and conventions. It is invaluable for finding public and private transit, tours, or watercraft that serve people with mobility limitations.

Advocates for Better Communication

New York League for the Hard of Hearing
71 W. 23rd St.
New York, NY 10010
(212) 741-7650 or (212) 255-1932 (TTY)

To make it easy to request assistive devices from hotels, Self-Help for Hard of Hearing People, Inc. has prepared a "Hotel Accommodations Request Card" to be mailed once you have a confirmed reservation. On it you should also indicate date and time of arrival and departure, and confirmation number. You can order these request cards free of charge from the above address. Enclose a self-addressed stamped envelope.

American Diabetes Association

www.diabetes.org
(800) 342-2383

At the website, you can read about new government regulations regarding traveling with diabetes supplies, obtain useful packing tips, learn about how to deal with time-zone changes, and read other information specifically geared for traveling with diabetes.

DialysisFinder

www.DialysisFinder.com

DialysisFinder can help you locate dialysis units closest to you, or locate units as you travel within the United States. The service is free. Just type in your destination city, and DialysisFinder does the rest instantly. This site also has an excellent page of related links.

The International Travelers Point and Conversation Guide
ArnMoor Publishing
3956 Town Center Blvd., Suite 104
Orlando, FL 32837
(407) 855-5934

This pocket-sized booklet allows one to communicate through pictures. While designed primarily to overcome the barriers of foreign language, it is equally suitable for use by people with speech impairments, here or abroad. It covers six main topics (services, shopping, sports and entertainment, transportation, accommodation, and food items) and also provides thirteen pages of conversion tables. To order a copy, send $6.95 plus return shipping.

National Council on Disability
www.ncd.gov
Phone: (202) 272-2004 • TTY: (202) 272-2074 • Fax: (202) 272-2022

This government website has information on the Americans with Disabilities Act and the Air Carriers Access Act, as well as current information about where to file complaints.

Society for Accessible Travel & Hospitality (SATH)
www.sath.org
Phone: (212) 447-7284 • Fax: (212) 725-8253

SATH's mission is to promote awareness, respect, and accessibility for elderly travelers and those with disabilities. The website features travel tips and excellent articles on how to travel by air with a wheelchair, how to travel with mobility impairments, sight or hearing impairments, arthritis, diabetes, and kidney disease.

Traveling with Pets

Pets on the Go
www.petsonthego.com
Phone: (781) 934-7202

This is a website for the "jet set pet," devoted to people and pets who like to travel together. Sign up for the newsletter, read about pet-friendly accommodations, get information on pet travel insurance, read travel tips, and more.

TakeYourPet.com
www.takeyourpet.com
Phone: (800) 790-5455 • Fax: (303) 662-1241

This is the largest pet travel club in the United States. The website offers a free newsletter for news, tips, and information about traveling with any type of pet.

Healthy Travel

Travel Health Online
www.tripprep.com

This website requires you to register (for free). After doing so, you can access lots of high-quality, up-to-date health information about your destination, including required vaccines, health advisories, medical facilities, and emergency numbers. The site also has accurate and comprehensive information about common traveler ailments, and offers loads of traveler health advice.

The Wellness Concierge
www.mrfedin.com

What a great website. Hosted by Marlene Fedin, who calls herself "The Wellness Concierge," this information-laden website has articles about international health alerts; healthy travel on airplanes, in cars, and on ships; healthy eating on the road; eating out advice for dieters; how to sleep well on strange beds; travel medicine tips; a free newsletter; recommended reading; travel health links; and much more. I highly recommend this website for solid travel health advice.

Recommended Reading

Do's and Taboos around the World, by Roger E. Axtell

Combatting Air Terrorism, by Rodney Walls

The Complete Guide to Conducting Seminars at Sea, Mary Long

The Complete Idiot's Guide to RVing, by Brent Peterson

Europe through the Back Door, by Rick Steves

Have Dog Will Travel, by Barbara Whitaker

The Packing Book, by Judith Gilford

Plane Insanity: A Flight Attendant's Tales of Sex, Rage, and Queasiness at 30,000 Feet, by Elliott Hester

Safe Travel in Bear Country: Safe Camping, Hiking and Fishing, by Gary Brown

Smart Packing, by Susan Foster

Travel Safe: Using Your Head As Well As Your Feet, by Cliff Terry

Travel Wise, Smart and Light, by Mary Nell York

Traveling On Your Own, Eleanor Berman

World's Most Dangerous Places, by Robert Young

Worst-Case Scenario Survival Handbook, by Joshua Piven, David Borgenicht, David Concannon, Brenda Brown

Worst-Case Scenario Survival Handbook: Travel, by Joshua Piven and David Borgenicht

Donate for Peace

I am donating a portion of the profits from this book to the International Institute for Peace through Tourism (IIPT), a not-for-profit organization dedicated to fostering and facilitating tourism initiatives that contribute to international understanding and cooperation, an improved quality of environment, and the preservation of heritage. Through these initiatives, IIPT is helping to bring about a peaceful and sustainable world.

If you would like to find out more about this terrific organization, visit their website at www.iipt.org. If you would like to make a tax-deductible contribution, send it to:

International Institute for Peace through Tourism
Fox Hill 13 Cottage Club Road
Stowe, Vermont 05672

For more information, contact IIPT at:

Phone: 802-253-2658
Fax: 802-253-2645
Email: conference@iipt.org